What the Bible Really Says about

Hell

by John D. Clark Sr., and "the boys"

What the Bible Really Says about Hell
© 2007 John David Clark, Sr.

ISBN-13: 978-1-934-78200-2

First Printing, 2007
Second Printing, 2024

cover design and graphics by Donna Nelson

John David Clark, Sr.
PO Box 99
Burlington, NC 27216–0099

Visit our websites:
www.GoingtoJesus.com
www.PastorJohnsHouse.com
www.SongsofRest.com
www.youtube.com/TheSpiritIstheWitness

Author's Notes

- In English, the singular and plural forms of "you" are identical. However, in biblical Hebrew and Greek, there are obvious differences. Therefore, to more perfectly convey the biblical writers' messages in verses where the English word "you" appears, I have italicized the "y" of all plural forms, such as *y*ou, *y*our, *y*ours, and *y*ourselves.

- Translations of Old and New Testament scriptures are my own. Following standard practice, whenever a word is added to the translation for clarification, that word is italicized. (See online: https://mypjv.com/)

- Conflicting rules exist as to how punctuation should be used, none of them being adequate for every situation. My Readers will find that I subscribe to a freer punctuation style. Of special note, I do not include within quotation marks any punctuation that is not a part of what is quoted. To do otherwise, in my opinion, leaves too much room for misrepresentation of the original author's intent.

*

DEDICATION

To faithful saints I have known, who lived their lives so
that they did not end up in Hell.
I thank them for their happy, holy examples.
And to those who are searching for answers to life's
most important issues
and want to know the truth about invisible things.

Table of Contents

Introduction

Introduction

"The boys" and I had not long begun our study of early American history when we read the diary of Mary Rowlandson, a young frontier wife and mother taken captive from her Lancaster, Massachusetts, home and held for ransom by Indians. Her devotion to God during the ensuing months and her prodigious knowledge of the Scriptures impressed us. And our admiration of her deepened as we read of her humble repentance for some relatively minor offenses in her former life, such as pipe-smoking and ingratitude for friends and the ordinary comforts of home, and of how sincerely she dedicated herself anew to God.

Mary was an exceptionally observant and perceptive woman. Her diary, written after she was ransomed by her husband from the Indians, includes insightful and detailed descriptions of the Indians' way of life. One night, she recorded how her captors danced wildly in the camp:

"There was [near] by a vacant house (deserted by the English before, for fear of the Indians). I asked them whether I might not lodge in the house that night, to which they answered, 'What, will you love English men still?' This was the dolefulest night that ever my eyes saw. Oh the roaring, and singing and dancing, and yelling of those black creatures in the night, which made the place a lively resemblance of hell."

As the boys and I were reading that section of Mary's diary, we fell into a discussion of how people in our culture typically imagine Hell. I pointed out to this small group of homeschoolers that, as a whole, Western society's concept of Hell from the time of the Middle Ages actually has its roots more in Pagan myth than in biblical truth. It is still true, for example, that when provoked by doctrines that displease them, many Christians condemn those teachings as "doctrines from Hell". Or they may respond to an especially atrocious deed as having been inspired by "demons from Hell". Yet, the notion that anything comes from Hell is non-biblical. The Devil and his angels came to earth from Heaven, not from Hell (cf. Rev. 12:7–12). The idea that something can come to earth from the underworld originated in classical mythology and was passed on to Western society through Christian leaders, such as Dante Alighieri in his epic poem, *The Divine Comedy*.

When I asked the boys if they would like to read Dante's *Divine Comedy*, they eagerly accepted the offer. Afterward, however, I had second thoughts. How could I justify exposing their impressionable young minds to such a powerful, godless myth-maker as Dante before they were established in the truth revealed in the Scriptures? I could not. I was loath to renege on my offer to read Dante with them, but I also knew that I could not foist on them Dante's powerful, mythological vision of the underworld without first making certain that they possessed a steady plumb line by which to judge his work. They needed a sure knowledge of what the Bible says about the place of damnation to which Dante would pretend to take them. That was the genesis of this study, and as it progressed, it proved to be more beneficial to us all than I expected. So, with confidence in the benefit of the enterprise, we deter-mined to pass along to you what we learned.

The statements and attitudes of godly biblical characters concerning the abode of the dead serve as a beacon for all who want the truth about life after death. We followed the light of that beacon wherever it took us, and where it eventually took us was to a better understanding of much more than Hell, for we gained in our journey a far deeper appreciation for both the love and the fear of God.

It seems odd that the study of Hell could inspire a deep care for others, but that is what we experienced. How could such a thing be? After all, love is perceived to be such a tender thing, and, by contrast, Hell is a place where tenderness can only be remembered, never experienced. Nevertheless, this study produced in us a sense of the abiding love and goodness of God that is directed toward mankind. To our happy surprise, this work proved to be more a story about God than about Hell, and we found that as we pursued the truth, it bore in us a fuller measure of the peaceful fruit of love and hope. It is humbly offered to you in the love of Christ, as a service to your faith, which love always produces an earnest hope for others' blessing and peace.

The boys and I greet you and wish for you only the best in Christ Jesus, the Son of God and only Savior.

John D. Clark Sr., and "the boys":
Elijah Clark, Aaron Nelson, Josiah Payne

Our Purpose

Our objective in this study was to find out what the Bible really says about the abode of the dead and to separate fact from fiction. No tradition, no belief, no opinion was immune from critical examination in the light of what we would find in the Bible.

To ancient people, including those of the Bible, the abode of the dead was not the place that modern men typically imagine it to be. For example, in our culture, a visit from a ghost is generally held to be a "spooky" experience. In the literature available from the ancient world, however, we do not typically find that to be the case. The ghost (or "shade") of a dead person returning to the land of the living was not necessarily frightful; it was merely a visit from a person who dwelt in another realm. The reason the witch of Endor screamed when she saw the deceased prophet Samuel coming toward her was not because she was afraid of ghosts, but because the appearing of Samuel revealed the identity of King Saul, who was there with her and who had decreed that all witches were to be put to death (1Sam. 28:9). It was a fear of the living, not the dead, that made her scream.

Additionally, although most ancient people did not understand Hell to be a fiery place of torment, they still did not view life in Hell as preferable to life on earth. In Homer's *Odyssey*, when the Greek hero Odysseus made his famous visit to Hades, his former comrade-in-arms, Achilles, told him, "I'd rather be a day-laborer on earth working for a man of little property than be lord of all the hosts of the dead" (Od. 11:489–491).[1] The ancients felt that way, not because they feared being tormented in flames, but because life on earth was just seen as a better place to live than Hell.

Abraham had been in Hell over a thousand years when Homer composed the *Odyssey*; yet, Jesus' words in John 8:56 suggest that Abraham's attitude toward life in Hell approximated Achilles'. He said, "Abraham was overjoyed that he might see my day, and he saw it, and rejoiced." Abraham's joy must have been inspired by the knowledge that Jesus would get him out of that place.

There are verses in the Old Testament which suggest an association between God's wrath and Hell, so we cannot say that Israel had no clue as to what lay beyond the grave for the wicked. The lack of clear information notwithstanding, no person in Israel desired to go to the place of the dead, for it was believed by all to be a less happy place to be than on earth. One exception to the rule of ancient characters not desiring to go to Hell was Job, who begged God to send him to Hell so that he could escape his earthly agonies (Job 14:13). How horrible must Job's suffering have been for him to plead with God to send him to the place to which all the living dreaded to go!

The Word "Hell"

In the Old Testament, Hell is referred to by several names, among them *Sheol* and *the Pit*. Hell is also called by other names in the New Testament, such as *Hades* and, again, *the Pit*. We will carefully examine all those terms, along with others, but we decided it was best for clarity's sake to use the word *Hell* for them all. As an example of our reasoning, we noticed that in Acts 2, Peter quoted

---

[1] See Appendix, "Using Ancient Myths".

Psalm 16:10, in which the Hebrew says, "You will not leave my soul in Sheol." Peter and the people to whom he was preaching spoke Hebrew, and Peter would no doubt have used the word *Sheol*, as David did. But Acts was written in the Greek language, and the author translated Peter's words with the Greek word for *Sheol*: "You will not leave my soul in Hades" (Acts 2:27). The author's choice of *Hades* for *Sheol* shows that he knew Hades was the place the Jews called Sheol. That is one example of many that I could use to show why in this book, we used the word *Hell* whenever *Sheol* and *Hades* are found in the Scriptures.

The Devil and Satan

Some have argued that the Devil is not Satan, but that notion is clearly contrary to the Scriptures. John wrote in Revelation 12:9, "The great Dragon was cast out [of Heaven], the ancient serpent who is called the Devil, and Satan, who deceives the whole world." So, in this work, we use both those names for the wicked, fallen cherub (cf. Ezek. 28:12–17) whom Isaiah called Lucifer (or "Light-bringer" – Isa. 14:12).

What the Bible Really Says about

Hell

by John D. Clark Sr., and "the boys"

Chapter One

Hell

WHERE IS HELL?

Jacob, Hannah, David, Job, Isaiah, Ezekiel, and other godly and wise people of the ancient world referred to Hell as being "down" from the surface of the earth. God, through Moses, did the same in Numbers 16:30, as did the Son of God before his first Advent (Ps. 30:3), as well as when he was here among us (Mt. 11:23). Jesus told his disciples that he would go down for three days into "the heart of the earth" (Mt. 12:40). His doing so fulfilled the prophecy that he would descend into Hell (Ps. 16:10). It was also revealed to Paul that before Jesus ascended into Heaven, he "descended into the lower parts of the earth" (Eph. 4:9).

======

The answer to the question, "Where is Hell?" is that Hell is "down", that is, beneath the earth's surface, somewhere in the heart of the earth.

IS "THE PIT" ANOTHER NAME FOR HELL?

Hell and the Pit are mentioned together in Psalm 30:3: "O LORD, you have brought up my soul from Hell; you restored me to life from the depths of the Pit!" (cf. Ps. 88:3–4a). And just as in David's time, death resulted in one's soul descending into Hell, so death resulted in descending into the Pit (e.g., Job 33:24; Ps. 88:4). The Pit is also said to be "down" (e.g., Ps. 30:3; 88:4; 143:7; Prov. 1:12; Ezek. 32:30).   When David spoke of the Pit being dug for the wicked (Ps. 94:13), common sense tells us that the digging was in a downward direction.   Also, the Pit is repeatedly said by Ezekiel to be "in the lower parts of the earth" (Ezek. 26:20; 31:14–18; 32:18), like Hell.

The Pit, also like Hell, has levels, and the wickedest men are cast into the lowest levels of it (Ps. 55:23).   And after he was crucified, the Son of God went there, too: "You have set me in the lowest pit, in the darkest of depths" (Ps. 88:6).   The Pit also has "sides" (Isa. 14:15; Ezek. 32:23), but we are given no further information about that.   Like Hell, the Pit has gates and is called a prison (Job 17:16; Isa. 24:22).   It is an unsavory place to which David did not look forward to going (cf. Ps. 69:15).

There is no acceptable worship in the Pit (Ps. 88:5b), for the souls there have been "cut off from God's hand" (Ps. 88:5), and God does not answer their cries.   David understood this and prayed, "To you I cry, O LORD my Rock! Do not be deaf to me, lest, if you are silent to me, I be like those who go down into the Pit!" (Ps. 28:1).   Those in the Pit are helpless (Ps. 88:4b), which is the same information we have concerning souls in the place called Hell.

======

The answer to our question, "Is the Pit another name for Hell?" is yes.

IS HELL ORGANIZED?

Especially in John's Revelation, we see an impressive orderliness in Heaven.   The same is seen in God's orderly week of creation, in the law of Moses, and in every other act of God. It is manifest that God is the Master of organization. Therefore, it should not surprise us to find that "the things under the earth" were also created in a well-organized manner.

The fact that Hell was originally divided into two distinct parts, Paradise and Torment, is the first indication that Hell is a well-organized place. The fact that there are degrees of suffering is another indication of a planned order in the lower parts of the earth. And as we mentioned, both Isaiah and Ezekiel speak of the "sides of the Pit". Ezekiel adds a fairly lengthy description of souls in Hell positioned in what appears to be a regimented manner, with sinners kept together according to their nationality (Ezek. 32:18–32), and according to their mightiness (Ezek. 32:23).

======

The answer to our question, "Is Hell organized?" is yes.

WHO IS IN CHARGE OF HELL?

Solomon said, "Hell lies open before the LORD" (Prov. 15:11), and Job said, "Hell is naked before Him" (Job 26:6). Reason tells us that if Hell is open and naked before God, then He knows everything that happens there and knows everyone in it, and that implies control. But in 1Samuel 2:6, Hannah settled the issue when she was moved by the Spirit to say, "The LORD kills and restores to life; He brings down to Hell and raises up." Later in Israel's history, David and Ezekiel agreed with Hannah, that God is the One who casts people down into Hell (Ps. 55:23; Ezek. 31:16).

David made it plain, as did Job and Solomon, that if anyone thinks he can hide from God in Hell, he is mistaken. He wrote in Psalm 139:8, "If I ascend to Heaven, you are there. Or if I make my bed in Hell, behold, you are there." The LORD Himself said of certain wicked people, "Though they dig into Hell, there my hand will take hold of them, and though they ascend into Heaven, from there will I bring them down" (Amos 9:2). Another bit of biblical information indicating that God's power over Hell is absolute is found in Hosea 13:14, where God says of the righteous dead, "I will ransom them from the power of Hell; I will redeem them from death." Finally, in the revelation given to John, Jesus declared conclusively, "I have the keys of death and of Hell" (Rev. 1:18).

Satan has nothing to do with Hell. In fact, he will never even go there. At the close of this age, Satan will not be thrown into Hell but will be cast directly into the Lake of Fire (Rev. 20:10), which is not Hell but a place into which Hell itself will ultimately be cast (Rev. 20:14). This is how God will destroy Hell forever; He will cast it into the Lake of Fire. When Satan was not in Heaven, as he often was before Jesus came, he spent his time "going to and fro in the earth, and from walking up and down in it" (Job 1:7; 2:2). And he is still doing that, according to the apostle Peter's warning to the saints: "*Your adversary, the Devil, is walking about like a roaring lion, seeking whom he may devour*" (1Pet. 5:8b). When the Devil was banished from Heaven after Jesus ascended and was glorified, he was cast down to earth, not into Hell (Rev. 12:7–12). There is no indication that he has dwelt anywhere but on earth since then.

At the end of this age, there will be a new Heaven and a new earth (Rev. 21:1), and one may ask, What will become of this present Heaven and earth? Jesus only told us that this Heaven and earth will pass away (Mt. 24:35), but Peter provided some details about how that will happen: "The heavens will pass away with a roar, and the elements will be consumed with burning heat, and the earth and the works that are in it will be burned up. The heavens, being on fire, will be destroyed, and the elements, consumed with heat, will be dissolved" (2Pet. 3:10, 12). Such complete destruction can only be accomplished by God, and so, His control over Hell is again confirmed.

======

The answer to our question, "Who is in charge of Hell?" is that God is in charge.

WHO GOES DOWN INTO HELL?

We find in the Bible that people must die in order to go to Hell. Living people do not go there.[2] This has been the case from the very beginning, for God revealed through Ezekiel that people from ancient times were in Hell (Ezek. 26:20). This requirement of death in order to descend into Hell is shown in Revelation 6:8, where Hell is described as *following* death, not preceding it. It is not surprising to find David poetically describing dead men's bones, scattered around a grave, as lying at the mouth of Hell (Ps. 141:7). So, the biblical evidence leads us to conclude that no person enters into Hell automatically or by his own will; God first ends a person's earthly life (Dt. 32:39) and then sends that soul into Hell. This biblical truth shows that Homer's story of the hero Odysseus visiting Hell while he was still alive is only a myth.

---

[2] The leaders of the great wilderness rebellion against Moses are the only exceptions mentioned in the Bible (Num. 16:18–33).

That having been said, the only way to completely answer the question "Who goes down into Hell?" is to divide the answer into two periods of time: the time before Jesus ascended into Heaven to offer himself to God for our sins, and afterward.

Paradise and Torment

Jesus' parable of the rich man and the beggar Lazarus (Lk. 16:19–31) revealed that Hell, at that time, was divided into two parts: Paradise for the righteous and Torment for the wicked. After the rich man and the beggar died, they both found themselves in Hell, but in different parts of it; the beggar was taken to Paradise, Jesus said, while the rich man was cast into Torment. The parable also revealed that in Hell, the righteous and the wicked could see and talk to each other, though they were separated by a wide, uncrossable gulf. So, before the New Testament began in Acts 2, both the righteous and the wicked descended into Hell when they died.

In Genesis 37:35, righteous Jacob said, "I will go down mourning into Hell, to my son." Thinking that his son Joseph was dead, Jacob assumed that Joseph had gone down into Hell and that he would join Joseph in Hell when he died. When God used the witch to bring up the prophet Samuel out of Hell, Samuel rebuked the backslidden King Saul and told him that he and his sons would be killed the next day and would join him in Hell (1Sam. 28:7–20), though he no doubt knew that Saul would be in Torment, not in Paradise with him. In Psalm 18:4–5, Christ spoke through David and prophesied that he, too, would go to Hell when he died: "Cords of death encompassed me; cords of Hell enveloped me; snares of death confronted me." It is important to note that although Jesus was sinless, he also went down into Hell when he died.[3] Lastly, we find the righteous but ailing King Hezekiah weeping and crying out, "I must enter the gates of Hell. I am deprived of the remainder of my years" (Isa. 38:10). Such verses make it clear that the righteous who lived before the New Testament went down into Hell when they died.

Of the wicked, Job said, "Drought and heat snatch away snow waters; Hell, those who have sinned" (Job 24:19). And King David agreed that "wicked men shall be turned into Hell" (Ps. 9:17a), and he warned his children that immorality would take them into the depths of Hell (Prov. 5:3–5; 7:27; 9:18). But how much he and Job understood about how Hell was organized is not clear. All that we can say is that everyone seemed to know that after death, they would descend into the heart of the earth.

After Jesus Ascended

The question "Who goes down into Hell?" has now been partly answered. In the ages before the New Testament, as the righteous were dying, they would say only, "I will go to my fathers in peace" (cf. Gen. 15:15); no righteous person who lived before the New Testament ever said on his deathbed, "I am going to be with the Lord." It is only in the New Testament writings that we read such statements as "to leave this home of the body [is] to be at home with the Lord" (2Cor. 5:8).

Before the New Testament was inaugurated, the righteous were carried by angels into the part of Hell called Paradise (Lk. 16:22), and the wicked were taken by angels into the part of Hell called Torment (Mt. 13:41–42; 49–50). Since Jesus instituted the New Testament, however,

---

[3] See Appendix, "The Spirits in Prison".

only evildoers are taken into Hell, for the upright are now taken into the presence of the Lord in Heaven. This was an extraordinary change, that the Paradise portion of Hell was removed from the heart of the earth and transferred to Heaven, "where Christ is sitting at God's right hand" (Col. 3:1). But when did that transfer take place?

It is only Jesus' ascension that explains it. Jesus must have transferred Paradise into Heaven when he ascended to his Father and was glorified. This transfer of Paradise from Hell into Heaven was the basis for Paul's teaching, that when Jesus ascended on high, he "took captivity captive" (Eph. 4:8). Paul's words imply that the righteous souls in Hell, even though in Paradise, were held in captivity until the Messiah came and delivered them. That would explain why Abraham (and others like him in Hell) were so happy to see the day of God's Messiah come. Abraham's joy implies an awareness on his part that Jesus' mission included delivering him from the place from which he could see so many souls in agony and hear their miserable cries for help.

Everything Depended on Jesus

The New Testament is very clear that Jesus paid the price for all the sins of mankind, both the sins committed before he came to earth and those committed afterward (Rom. 3:25; Heb. 9:15). Every mercy that God granted to repentant sinners before Christ came was granted only on the condition that Christ would come and pay the price for those sins.[4] Everything depended on Jesus. Faith in Christ Jesus is the only means of salvation for all people, whether or not they lived on earth before he did. Abraham and other righteous souls like him in Paradise somehow

---

[4] See Appendix, "New Testament Mercy".

sensed that Jesus was the key to their hope for eternal life, even if they did not know how Jesus would go about securing that hope. And they were right. If Jesus had not paid the price for man's guiltiness before God, no one's sins would ever have been washed away. There has never been a sin blotted out of God's book by anything except the blood of the sinless Lamb of God.

Foretold

God's transfer of Paradise from the heart of the earth to Heaven was foretold by the prophets, even though the prophets did not understand those prophecies. Through Zechariah, for example, the Father said to the Son, "By the blood of your covenant, I have released your prisoners from the Pit in which is no water" (Zech. 9:11). In Isaiah, too, we find the Father speaking to the Son: "I will give you for a covenant for the people, for a light of the nations, to open the eyes of the blind, to bring prisoners out of the dungeon, those who sit in darkness out of the prison house" (Isa. 42:6b–7). And again, "In the acceptable time, I will answer you, and in the day of salvation, I will help you and give you for a covenant of the people, saying to the prisoners, 'Come forth!' And to those in darkness, 'Show yourselves!'" (Isa. 49:8a, 9a). And after the Son came to earth and was anointed with power and sent by God to "do good and heal all who were oppressed by the Devil", he went on the Sabbath day into his hometown synagogue, where he read from the scroll of the prophet Isaiah: "The Spirit of the Lord GOD is upon me, for the LORD has anointed me to proclaim good news to the poor. He has sent me to bind up the broken-hearted, to declare liberty to those held captive, and freedom to those in prison" (Isa. 61:1; Lk. 4:16–18). Everyone in Hell was a prisoner, whether in Paradise or Torment, but because the righteous had a promise from God that they would be delivered, they were called "prisoners of hope" (Zech. 9:12), while those in Torment were prisoners with no hope. Jesus' release of the righteous prisoners in Hell is proof of the Father's care for those who trust in Him.[5]

The Wicked Dead in the New Testament

The apostles said almost nothing about where the wicked go when they die under this covenant, but we can make some deductions based on the scant information we have. We know that Hell still exists because in Revelation, John spoke of people being in Hell at the time of the end (Rev. 20:13). From that, we may conclude that (1) people are in Hell now just as they were before the New Testament began, and (2) people will be in Hell until the end of this age. Furthermore, since we know that when Jesus ascended, he transferred Paradise and its righteous souls into Heaven, we also know that the dead whom John saw in Hell in Revelation were the wicked dead.

======

The complete answer to the question, "Who goes down into Hell?" is that before Jesus ascended into Heaven to offer his atoning sacrifice to God, everyone went down into Hell when they died, either to Paradise or to Torment. However, since Jesus transferred Paradise into Heaven, only the wicked go down into Hell now when they die.

---

[5] God is willing to set His prisoners free (Ps. 146:7; 69:33) but Satan has never willingly released any prisoner of his (cf. 2Tim. 2:26; Isa. 14:17).

CAN ANYONE ESCAPE HELL?

Job asked, "If a man die, shall he live again?" (Job 14:14). The answer, as Job well knew, was no – unless God decided to bring someone back to life. Both Job and Hezekiah described Hell as having "bars" or "gates" (Job 17:16; Isa. 38:10), and Jesus, too, mentioned "the gates of Hell" (Mt. 16:18). Job knew that apart from an extraordinary work of God, being in Hell was a permanent condition: "As a cloud dissipates and goes away, so he who goes down to Hell does not come up" (Job 7:9). In Ecclesiastes 3:14, Solomon declared that whatever God does is eternal and that no one can change it. That being true, and since sending men into Hell is one of the things God does, we know that no one can undo it. The wisest thing that a man can do in response to what God does is to fear what God will choose to do with him, for whatever God chooses to do with anyone is forever.

Still, ancient righteous people hoped in God. Job, for example, knew that God would never forsake those who trust in Him, even if they were dead and in Hell: "I know that my Redeemer lives, and in the end, he shall stand upon the earth! And afterward, when this skin they have destroyed, though without my flesh, I shall see God" (Job 19:25–26). Job believed that just as the Creator had power to send men into Hell, so He had power to deliver men out of it. Much later, God promised to ransom the upright from Hell: "I will ransom them from the power of Sheol; I will redeem them from death. O Death, where are your plagues? Where is your sting, O Sheol?" (Hos. 13:14a). But long before He made that promise, Job believed that it was possible for the dead to be helped, for he prayed, "Oh, that you would hide me in Hell and conceal me until your anger is passed, that you would appoint me a time and re-member me!" (Job 14:13).

Jesus' Escape

Paul was speaking of Jesus' escape from Hell when he wrote that before Jesus ascended into Heaven, he de-scended into the lower parts of the earth (Eph. 4:9). In Psalm 142:7, the Son of God prayed, "Bring my soul out of the dungeon so that I might praise your name!" And from Psalm 71:20–21, he prophesied again, "You who have shown me many and grievous troubles will bring me back to life and cause me to rise again from the depths of the earth. You will increase my greatness and comfort me again." And again he declared, "God will ransom my soul from the power of Hell, for He will receive me!" (Ps. 49:15). And in Psalm 86:13, the Son, speaking of his fu-ture resurrection, gave thanks to God, saying, "You have delivered my soul from the depths of Hell!"

Let's Pause a Minute to Honor God

It is only right that we study the Scriptures and weigh their meaning; at the same time, we must avoid the pitfall of pride, lest our study become merely an academic exer-cise. It is easy to dig past the treasure. Many a scholar has prided himself on the huge pile of excavated earth on his shelves instead of being humbled by the love of God expressed in the suffering and glory of Jesus. We are loved by God! That glorious truth canopies everything the Bible has to say, and those who know the Bible best feel it most. Too often, however, that is not the case. Let us strive to get the point as we learn new things about Hell: Jesus suffered and died to save us from that awful place; we don't have to go there!

The goal of all learning should always be to imitate the life of Christ Jesus because *he* is the point. He is "the way, and the truth, and the life" (Jn. 14:6). When we truly understand life, we love Jesus and bow in awe at the terrible suffering he endured to bring us eternal life. And we value as well the suffering of the Father in Heaven, who restrained Himself as His Son was abused and cruelly slain by men. Both the Father and the Son paid a price of great, innocent pain for our salvation. We have hope of eternal life because of the willingness of both the Son *and* the Father to suffer. We mentioned previously these compelling words of the Father to His Son through Zechariah: "By the blood of your covenant, I have released your prisoners from the Pit in which is no water." But too often, such scriptures remind us only of the suffering of the Son and not of the Father, whose heart was bleeding when He "bowed the heavens" to be close to Jesus during his great agony (Ps. 18:9). So, we give praise and honor to the Father and the Son for the pain they endured to bring to us "so great a salvation."

All Things Are Possible with God

As to the question "Can anyone escape Hell?" the answer is found in a phrase from Jesus: "With men it is impossible, but not with God, for all things are possible with God." God did bring Jesus up out of Hell, and then by him, the righteous souls in Paradise were taken from Hell into Heaven.

But to answer the question completely, we must consider the final end of the wicked. According to John's Revelation, the final destination of those who are now in Hell will be a place far worse than Hell. Here is John's description of their dreadful, final judgment from God:

"Death and Hell gave up the dead who were in them, and they were judged, each one according to their deeds. And Death and Hell were cast into the Lake of Fire. This is the Second Death, the Lake of Fire. And if anyone was not found written in the Book of Life,[6] he was cast into the Lake of Fire" (Rev. 20:13–15).

======

The answer to the question, "Can anyone escape Hell?" is no. However, everyone in Hell will leave it, in God's time. The righteous left Hell with Jesus to go into Heaven, and the wicked will leave Hell at the Final Judgment to go into the Lake of Fire.

IS HELL THE LAKE OF FIRE?

There are a few similarities between Hell and the Lake of Fire. In Luke 16, the rich man in Hell begged Abraham for a drop of water to cool his tongue, saying, "I am in agony in this flame" (16:24), and a similar fiery torment exists in the Lake of Fire. It is, after all, the "Lake *of Fire*". Jesus used the phrase "weeping and gnashing of teeth" only in reference to the Lake of Fire (Mt. 24:51; Lk. 13:28), but some degree of "weeping and gnashing of teeth" must also be the inconsolable condition of the wicked dead in Hell. So, the similarity between Hell and the Lake of Fire is the element of fire itself, but beyond that, similarities are hard to find.

One of the differences between these two places of the damned was revealed by Jesus when he said that the ungodly "will be cast out into outer darkness" (Mt. 8:12; cf.

----

[6] This includes people whose names were once in God's Book of Life, but who were disobedient and had their names "blotted out" (cf. Ex. 32:32–33; Rev. 3:5).

22:13 and 25:30).   With the phrase "outer darkness", the
Lord presents us with an oft-overlooked element of the
Lake of Fire, namely, its flames produce no light.   Unlike
Hell, the Lake of Fire is a place of absolute darkness.
Psalm 49:19 tells us that the damned in that place "will
never see light."   The "blackness of eternal darkness" of
which Jesus, Peter, and Jude spoke (Mt. 22:13; 2Pet. 2:17;
Jude 13) is a reference to the Lake of Fire, not to Hell, be-
cause in Hell, as Jesus said, the damned can see (Lk.
16:23).

To John on the Isle of Patmos, it was also revealed that
the Lake of Fire burns with brimstone (Rev. 19:20; 20:10;
21:8).   Brimstone is sulfur, and anyone who has ever had
fumes from burning sulfur enter his nostrils knows that it
has a suffocating effect.   So, in addition to the agony of
burning, those in the Lake of Fire will suffer with a feeling
of being smothered.   And there is more.   In Jesus' parable
of the condemned wedding guest, the king commanded,
"Bind his feet and hands, take him away, and cast him into
outer darkness" (Mt. 22:13a).   This binding of hands and
feet suggests the absence of choice, so that the damned are
not able even to change body positions.   In the Lake of
Fire, the wicked will suffer excruciating pain in suffocating blackness and be bound so tightly they cannot move,
forever.

Also, unlike Hell, the Lake of Fire was created as a
place from which there is no hope of ever coming out.   It
is the eternal home of the damned.   Sinners be tormented there "night and day forever and ever" (Rev.
20:10).   It is a place to which no one wants to go, and to
which no godly person wants anyone else to go.

======

The answer to our question, "Is Hell the Lake of Fire?" is no. Hell is the holding pen for the wicked dead until the Final Judgment. Then, the wicked will be taken out of Hell to be judged, and, after that, they will be cast into the Lake of Fire, along with Hell itself (Rev. 20:14).

ARE THERE DEGREES OF SUFFERING FOR THE DAMNED?

Jesus told Pontius Pilate that the sin of the Jews in turning him over to the Romans was greater than Pilate's sin in holding the Son of God prisoner. The Lord had already taught his followers that some commandments of God were weightier than others (Mt. 23:23), and certainly, greater transgressions demand greater punishment, for God's judgment of people is always said to be based upon their deeds (e.g., Jn. 5:28–29; Rom. 2:5–10). That there are degrees of torment was only suggested in the Old Testament, with such phrases as "the depths of Hell" (Dt. 32:22; Ps. 86:13; Prov. 9:18), but Jesus made the truth plain when he said that it will be more tolerable for some sinners on the Day of Judgment than for others (e.g., Mt. 10:15; 11:24). Jesus said that "the servant who knew his master's will but did not prepare nor do his will shall receive many stripes, but the one who didn't know and did things worthy of stripes shall receive just a few. From everyone to whom much is given, much will be required" (Lk. 12:47–48a). For that reason, James cautioned his readers not to pursue positions of authority because those who occupy such places in the kingdom of God will receive stricter judgment (Jas. 3:1).

Jesus also said that all sin could be forgiven except blasphemy of the holy Ghost (Mt. 12:31–32), but there have been sins which provoked God so greatly that He swore He would never forgive them. In Isaiah's day, for example, some in Israel mocked God's gracious call for repentance, which provoked Him to such wrath that He swore their sin would never be forgiven (Isa. 22:12–14).

======

The answer to the question, "Are there degrees of suffering for the damned?" is yes.

IS HELL A NATURAL PLACE OR A SPIRITUAL PLACE?

If Hell is a spiritual place, then the question must be asked, How can living people, still in their flesh, fall into it? as in Numbers 16:30–33, where God opened the earth to swallow up Dathan and Abiram after they led a revolt against Moses. The Bible specifically states that those rebels fell alive into Hell. And Dathan and Abiram are not the only examples of people in a physical body being cast alive into fires of damnation. We are told in Revelation 19:20 that when Jesus returns to reign on earth for a thousand years, the Beast and the False Prophet will be "thrown alive into the Lake of Fire." And in Psalm 55:15, the Spirit of Christ prayed through David that certain of his enemies would be cast alive into Hell. These are "those under the earth" (Phip. 2:10; cf. Rev. 5:3). But if Hell is a natural place, then how is it that departed souls go there? That is an unanswerable question.

That the souls of men go into Hell is clear from scriptures such as these: "You will not leave my soul in Hell" (Ps. 16:10a), and "God will ransom my soul from the power of Hell" (Ps. 49:15a). And while Solomon mentioned saving a soul from Hell (Prov. 23:14), he never said anything about saving a body from it. God created man from dirt, and when man sinned, God said that man would return to dirt. But that was said only of man's body. The life that God breathed into Adam's earthly body was not made from dirt, and no man's spirit has ever become dirt after he died. The spirit of man lives on after the body returns to dirt. That is why this study of Hell is even worth taking the time to do.

God can certainly make exceptions to any natural law. He kept Jesus, Moses, and Elijah alive without food or water for forty days (Mt. 4:2; Ex. 24:18; 1Kgs. 19:8). And Moses did this at least twice (Dt. 9:11–18). So, regardless of the conclusion to which reason and the Scriptures would lead us, if God chooses to have a transgressor to suffer in Hell in an earthly body, He will do so. There is nothing which binds God to a certain course of action. I am just pointing out the fact that, apart from a miracle, no one can live in Hell or in the Lake of Fire in a natural, human body.

All things considered, the conclusion that seems most reasonable is that Hell is a spiritual place. Natural law dictates that the earthly, physical bodies of those whom God casts alive into Hell or the Lake of Fire cannot survive there for long. Physical bodies require physical sustenance. So, earthly bodies cast alive into Hell must certainly die quickly, being in a place where there is not so much as a drop of water. As a rule, however, a natural body must die before the soul enters into Hell.

======

The answer to the question, "Is Hell a natural place or a spiritual place?" is that it appears to be a place for spirits. At the same time, however, it is said to be in the heart of the earth, which is a physical location.

WHAT DO PEOPLE IN HELL KNOW?

When people leave this life, many things become plain to them which they did not believe while here on earth. There are no atheists in Hell. All the dead know that God exists and that they are in His hands. They know the certainty of the Final Judgment; they know that Jesus is God's Son and that he is Lord of all; and they understand the truth, such as how they should have lived and what they needed from God in order to escape damnation. There is nothing the dead can do to change anything, as much as most of them would like to, but now without flesh covering their bodies, the fleshly nature that blinded them is no longer an obstacle to seeing what is right.

The dead also know one another, regardless of when in history they lived. Abraham lived two thousand years before Jesus' time, but the rich man in Jesus' parable who died and was carried into Hell knew who Abraham was when he saw him far off in Paradise (Lk. 16:19–31). Kings from every nation who were in Hell when the king of Babylon went there, many no doubt having died long before he did, knew who he was as soon as he entered into Hell with them (Isa. 14:9–10).

When Solomon said, "The dead know nothing" (Eccl. 9:5), he meant that they know nothing of what is happening "under the sun", that is, on earth. The dead do not become angels to watch over us, as some people think. They do not know what is happening to their friends or loved ones and are ignorant of national triumphs or tragedies. The book of Ecclesiastes is a description of life "under the sun", a phrase he used twenty-nine times in twelve short chapters, and the dead know nothing of this life. Here under the sun, the living know nothing about the world of the dead, except what God has revealed, and the dead, if

God would allow it, could teach the living much about where they are, which is no longer under the sun. The rich man in Jesus' parable remembered his previous life "under the sun", and still had feelings for his loved ones. He begged Abraham to send someone from Paradise to his brothers, to warn them not to live as he had lived, but God would not allow that to happen.

========

The answer to the question, "What Do People in Hell Know?" is that although they do remember their previous life on earth, they know nothing about that life beyond the moment of their death. However, they are now acquainted with eternal, spiritual realities which they may or may not have believed in before they died.

DO THE DEAD STILL HAVE BODIES?

According to Jesus' parable of the rich man in Hell (Lk. 16:20–31), the dead have eyes (v. 23); the dead have tongues that can sense thirst (v. 24); the dead have fingers (v. 24); the dead have bosoms (v. 23); the dead can speak and hear (vv. 24–26); the dead can feel pain (v. 24); the dead can remember (v. 27); and the dead have feelings of fear and of compassion for their loved ones still on earth (v. 28). And more has been revealed by other men of God. Paul said that the dead have knees as well as tongues (Phip. 2:10–11), and Paul and John both suggested that the dead have feet and legs (Rom. 14:10; Rev. 20:12). And yet, the rich man of Jesus' parable had left his physical body back on earth, where it decayed. Obviously, the dead have human form, but that form is not made of the kind of flesh they had while on earth. As Paul said,

"There is a physical body, and there is a spiritual body" (1Cor. 15:39, 44).

When God brought the prophet Samuel up out of Hell to rebuke King Saul, Samuel had a recognizable form. Seeing him, the witch who brought up Samuel screamed, which prompted King Saul to ask her what she was looking at. She answered first that she saw "gods" ascending out of the earth, which might have been angels returning from Hell after carrying souls into either Paradise or Torment. Then the terrified woman added, "An old man is coming up, and he is covered with a robe," and from her description, Saul knew that it was Samuel.

======

The answer to our question, "Do the dead still have bodies?" is yes, but they are spiritual, not fleshly.

WHAT CAN THOSE IN HELL DO?

In Psalm 6:5, the psalmist wrote, "In death, there is no remembrance of you; in Hell, who praises you?" Here, as in other places in the Bible, the word "remembrance" refers to acceptable sacrifices for sins, reminding God of His promise to forgive. For example, Hebrews 10:3, speaking of the sacrifices God commanded in the law, says, "In those sacrifices, remembrance of sins is made [before God] each year." This included the incense burning that God commanded: "The man shall bring his wife to the priest, and he shall bring her offering for her. . . . It is a memorial offering bringing iniquity to remembrance" (Num. 5:15).

So, in saying there is no remembrance of God among the dead, David was not saying that those in Hell were unable to remember God. They certainly did remember

God; however, they could not worship God as His law demanded at that time, with animal sacrifices, holy days, circumcision, water-cleansing rituals, etc.

It is equally true in this New Testament that in Hell there is no worship of God such as He demands. Jesus described what would be the only acceptable form of New Testament worship: "An hour is coming, and now is, when true worshippers will worship the Father spiritually and truly, for the Father is searching for such people to worship Him. God is a spirit, and those who worship Him must worship in spirit and in truth" (Jn. 4:23–24). That is impossible for anyone in Hell now because all the righteous have been moved to Heaven, and only the wicked remain. There are many true confessions being made in Hell because everyone in Hell, like the rich man in Luke 16, is compelled by their horrible suffering to acknowledge their sins, but there is no holy Spirit in Hell to cleanse them and make their pleas acceptable to God.

Paul taught that Christ within us is our "hope of glory" (Col. 1:27). Those in Hell cannot have Christ living within them, and so, they have no hope. If someone is in Hell who once received the Spirit of Christ while on earth, it has left them, and it may have done so even before they died. Most of the souls in Hell never received the Spirit. However, there are children of God in Hell who received the Spirit while on earth, but they went astray and never repented, and were cast into Hell at the end of their earthly lives. They are "reprobate", as Paul put it, for Christ no longer dwells within them (2Cor. 13:5).

From at least the tragic story of Aaron's two foolish sons in Leviticus 10, and throughout the rest of the Bible, we are repeatedly warned that worship is acceptable only if it is according to God's will. Then, another reason there is no acceptable worship in Hell is that God no longer communicates His will to the dead. God has never demanded anything of dead men. Even those to whom the law of Moses was given were made dead to the law when they died (Rom. 7:1). For all who die, all deeds are done, and their judgment is set. God does not answer their prayers. Prayers on earth that receive no response from God are a warning; they are an earthly foretaste of Hell. A truly godly life is characterized by receiving responses from God to prayer (Isa. 58:6–9a; 1Jn. 3:22), and such communion with God is an earthly foretaste of Heaven.

Hezekiah joined his voice with others concerning what souls in Hell can and cannot do when he said, "Hell does not offer you thanks; death does not praise you, and those who descend to the Pit do not hope for your truth. A living man, one who is alive, he will praise you, as I do this day" (Isa. 38:18–19a). It is only among the living that praises are acceptably offered, and the Psalmist took full advantage of the opportunity to do so: "I will give you thanks in the great assembly; with a mighty people will I praise you!" And he earnestly exhorted others to be so wise: "Exalt Him in the Assembly of the people, and praise Him in the council of elders," and "sing to the LORD a new song! Praise Him in the Assembly of the pious! Let Israel rejoice in his Maker; let the sons of Zion rejoice in their King. Let them praise His name in dance; with timbrel and lyre, let them sing to Him!" (Ps. 107:32; 149:1–3).

According to David, no one who died and entered the heart of the earth praised God. In Psalm 30:9, David sang, "Will the dust praise you? Will it make your truth known?" And David's friend Heman also asked, "Will departed spirits rise up and praise you? Will your lovingkindness be declared in the grave or your faithfulness in destruction?" (Ps. 88:10–11). But then, moved upon by the Spirit, David stated plainly, "The dead do not praise the LORD, nor any who go down to silence" (Ps. 115:17). So, it appears that in the Old Testament, neither the righteous dead in Paradise nor the unrighteous dead in Torment praised God in Hell. What a gloomy place it must have been!

No Distinctions

Solomon counseled those of his time to do with all their might whatever their hand found to do, "for there is no work, or planning, or knowledge, or wisdom in Hell where you are going" (Eccl. 9:10). The curse of God on fallen man on earth was that he must labor (Gen. 3:19), but in Hell, labor is a curse from which everyone is released forever. There are no occupations or professions, nor philosophical or scientific inquiry, nor clever invention, nor growing in knowledge. There are degrees of suffering in Hell, but there are few if any other distinctions among the damned. Earthly honors and positions are forever lost and mean nothing. No one will be intimidated by or ruled over by anyone else. Job said that in death, "the prisoners are at peace together; they do not hear the voice of the oppressor. The small and the great there are one, and the slave is free from his master" (Job 3:18–19). Some dead earthly kings in Hell offered this greeting to the once feared king of Babylon when he descended into it: "You have become weak as we! You are like us!" (Isa. 14:10). All his fearsome majesty and power were left on earth for some other proud fool to glory in; in Hell, there is no such glory.

To have God, by His Spirit, reach out to us, to teach us, to correct us, and to guide us in His holiness and truth is an element of earthly life that is so common that it is often taken for granted. Carnal men pant after earthly things rather than to humble themselves to ask for the free gift of God. God's great care for us, the living, so completely envelops all mankind that we cannot even imagine what it would be like to live in a place where He is altogether silent, but untold millions in Hell are experiencing that fearful reality right now. The Word of God no longer comes to them. It was with that knowledge that Isaiah confessed to God, "Those who descend to the Pit do not hope for your truth" (Isa. 38:18b). Anyone wanting to know the truth should be warned to seek it now, while it may be given. Isaiah pleaded with Israel to do so: "Seek the LORD while He may be found; call upon Him while He is near. Let the evil man forsake his way, and the wicked man, his thoughts, and return to the LORD, and He will have mercy on him, even to our God, for He will abundantly pardon" (Isa. 55:6–7). To be invited by God to seek Him is a precious gift.

The Church of Your Choice?

In Hell, then, without the Word of God, people are forever damned to call on God as best they can. Every person in Hell is earnestly crying out to God right now, in whatever way he thinks will best serve his own desperate purpose. Alas, they have no other choice, for the damned are liberated forever from the holy Spirit's strength to worship God as He demands. They are cursed forever to follow the advice of Christians who exhort believers today to "worship at the church of your choice." A fundamental part of the damnation of Hell is the absence of opportunity to worship God according to His will. Lost souls have no choice but to worship God as they think best, for it is the only way they can. Is that not the same as worshipping "at the church of your choice"? And is it not a foretaste of Hell to worship any way you choose? Damnation means that souls can worship *only* as they have chosen, for worship in the Spirit is no longer an option for them. That golden opportunity is only offered to the living.

For people to worship in the church of their choice is reminiscent of the comment at the end of the book of Judges describing the confusion of God's people at that time: "Every man did what was right in his own eyes." Not one of the Israelites who was living according to "what was right in his own eyes" understood the danger of choosing a church, so to speak. Every way that men have devised to worship God is vain; to God, denominations are abominations, and sects make wrecks of souls. Paul said that even the most devout forms of man's worship are worthless. "Such things," he wrote, "though having an appearance of wisdom in a self-willed religion, humility, and abuse of the body, are of no value to anyone in opposing gratification of the flesh" (Col. 2:23). Self-willed hearts do not understand that to live as it seems best to oneself is rebellion against God. At the time of the Judges, the wise were earnestly asking, as the wise are asking now, "What does God say?" for they know that in the end, what God has said will be the standard by which we will all be judged.

If ancient, rebellious Israelites never repented of wor-shipping God as they thought best, then it is certain that they are still worshipping God that way as they writhe in the tormenting flames of Hell. And, dear Reader, if you are worshipping God now in a way that you have chosen (the church of your choice) instead of the way God has ordained in Christ, then you are practicing for the way you will worship forever in torment.

No man has ever had the right, the authority, or permission to worship God as he thinks is best. Throughout the Bible, the death penalty hung over the head of anyone among God's people who dared to worship in a way that God had not ordained (e.g., Lev. 10:1–2). Eternal damnation will be the reward for those who reject the way of Christ and worship and live only as they see fit. On them, God will have the last laugh: "Because I called, and you refused, because I stretched out my hand and no one regarded it, because you disdained all my counsel and did not want my reproof, I will also laugh at your calamity. I will mock when your terror comes. . . . Then they will call on me, but I will not answer. They will seek me early, but they will not find me, forasmuch as they hated knowledge and did not choose the fear of the LORD. . . . They will eat the fruit of their own way, and they will be glutted with their own devices" (excerpts, Proverbs 1). In ancient Athens, Paul declared that God, in ages past, tolerated some errors in worship but that since the time God's Son gave his life for man's sins, "God commands all men everywhere to repent" (Acts 17:30) and learn to do things His way.

The next time you see a sign or bumper sticker that reads, "Worship at the Church of Your Choice", know that you are being invited to enjoy a little bit of Hell on earth.

God Must Choose Us

Without divine help, man cannot recognize and choose the right way (Mt. 19:25–26); he does not possess such wisdom. "But wisdom, where is it found?" asked Job,

"And where is the place of understanding? Man does not know its worth, for it is not found in the land of the living. The deep says, 'It is not in me.' And the sea says, 'It is not with me.' Fine gold cannot be given for it, nor can its price be weighed out in silver. . . . Yea, wisdom, from where does it come? And where is the place of understanding? It is concealed from the eyes of all living; hidden even from the fowl of Heaven. Abaddon and Death say, 'With our ears have we heard talk of it.' God grants understanding of its way, for He knows its place. . . . Then He said to man, 'Behold! Fear the Lord, that is wisdom, and to turn from evil to understanding!'" (excerpts, Job 28).

If a person believes what Job said, he understands that if wisdom "is not found in the land of the living," then the wisest of men are unable to find it. A truly wise man confesses the uselessness of his wisdom and puts his trust in God, while there is still hope, to guide him into truth. The path to wisdom is the path of humble supplication to God for help, but that path is hidden from the proud and worldly-wise, and Jesus rejoiced in that: "I thank you, Father," he said, "because you have hidden these things from the wise and prudent, and revealed them to babes. Yes, Father, for such was pleasing in your sight" (Mt. 11:25–26).

God must choose us (Jn. 15:16) and draw us to the right way (Jn. 6:44), the way of the Spirit, which Jesus made possible for us with his sacrificial death. Otherwise, we cannot attain to it. Man cannot even guess what is right about God; it is hidden, and no man possesses the ability to find it. We must be invited and then led into the knowledge of God.

======

The answer to the question, "What can those in Hell do?" is, not much. They are doomed to suffer helplessly forever, and to worship in the way of their choice.

Chapter Two
The Lake of Fire:
Gehenna, Tophet, and the Second Death

IS GEHENNA ANOTHER NAME FOR HELL?

The word *Gehenna* has a history as intriguing as it is obscure. In the beginning of Israel's history as a nation, when Joshua and Eleazar were dividing the land of Canaan among the tribes, there lived, or had lived, a man named Hinnom. We know nothing about him, not even whether or not he was an Israelite. All we know is that he had at least one son. Just once, late in Israel's history, "children of Hinnom" is mentioned (2Kgs. 23:10), but that could be a reference to Hinnom's grand-descendants and not to sons and daughters; so, whether Hinnom sired more than one son remains a mystery. The name of Hinnom's son, or of any other relative, also is unknown. The valley named for the son of Hinnom was at the base of the mountain upon which Jerusalem stood, to the south.

In the gospels, the valley was called Gehenna. About seventy-five percent of the time when Jesus referred to the place of punishment for the wicked dead, the word he used was neither *Sheol* nor *Hades*. It was instead the Hebrew word *Gehenna*, which is derived from the Old Testament name of the Valley of the Son of Hinnom.

It is significant that whenever Jesus mentioned people going into Gehenna, he always said they would be "cast into Gehenna"; he never says they would be cast *down* into Gehenna, as when he spoke of Hell (e.g., Mt. 11:23). This is because *Gehenna* was Jesus' term for the Lake of

Fire, not Hell, and the Lake of Fire is not down, in the heart of the earth. We learn from the book of Revelation that the Lake of Fire will continue forever, with tormented souls in it, but Jesus said this Heaven and earth, which includes the Hell beneath it, will be destroyed. He described the fire in Gehenna as "eternal" (Mt. 18:8), adding that it is an "unquenchable fire" (Mk. 9:45). These phrases cannot describe the fires of Hell, for Hell itself will be destroyed (Rev. 20:14).

Here are the eleven places where Jesus used the word Gehenna:

Matthew 5:22

"I say to *y*ou that everyone who is angry with his brother without cause will be liable to the Judgment, and whoever says to his brother, 'Raca!' will be accountable to the Council, and whoever says, 'You fool!' is in danger of fiery Gehenna."

Matthew 5:29–30 (= Matthew 18:9)

"If your right eye offends you, tear it out and cast it away from you! It is better for you that one of your members perish, and not that your whole body be cast into Gehenna. And if your right hand offends you, cut if off and cast it from you! It is better for you that one of your members perish, and not that your whole body be cast into Gehenna."

Mark 9:43–44 (= vv. 45–46 and 47–48)

"And if your hand should offend you, cut it off! It is better for you to enter into life maimed than with two hands to go into Gehenna, into the unquenchable fire, where their worm[7] does not die, and the fire is not quenched."

Matthew 10:28 (= Luke 12:4–5)
"Do not be afraid of those who kill the body but cannot kill the soul; rather, fear Him who is able to destroy both soul and body in Gehenna."

Matthew 23:15
"Woe to *you*, scribes and Pharisees! Hypocrites! *You* compass land and sea to make one convert, and when he is made, *you* make him twice as much a son of Gehenna as yourselves."

Matthew 23:33
"*You* snakes! *You* offspring of vipers! How can *you* escape the damnation of Gehenna?"

Looking into Gehenna

The similarity between Jesus' description of Gehenna and God's description of the Lake of Fire through the prophet Isaiah is remarkable. Jesus said, "It is better for you to enter into life maimed than with two hands to go into Gehenna, into the unquenchable fire, where their worm does not die, and the fire is not quenched." Compare that with this from Isaiah 66:24, keeping in mind that Isaiah is speaking of how things will be after the Final Judgment: "[God's saints] will go out [from worshipping God on the new earth] and look at the dead bodies of men

[7] The phrase "their worm does not die" (used by Isaiah, 66:24, and three times by Jesus, Mark 9:44, 46, 48) was in use in the mid-seventeenth century as a reference to a gnawing, guilty conscience. A collection of sayings concerning etiquette for young men, attributed to one Francis Hawkins, included this admonition: "Labour to keep alive in thy breast that little sparke of Celestial fire called Conscience, for Conscience to an evil man is a never dying worm, but unto a good man it's a perpetual feast."

who rebelled against me, for their worm will not die, and their fire will not be quenched, and they will be an abhorrence to all flesh." This cannot be a reference to Hell because according to John's revelation, Death and Hell will have already been destroyed.

The only place after the Final Judgment where the saints will find souls in torment is in the Lake of Fire, for that will be the only place left for them, since Hell itself was cast into it. This eternal Gehenna, the horrific Lake of Fire, will be located just outside the New Jerusalem (which will be on the new earth, cf. Rev. 22:14–15), as the Old Testament Gehenna was located just outside ancient Jerusalem. And as people could not avoid seeing Gehenna in ancient times when they came to Jerusalem, so God's people who visit the New Jerusalem will not be able to avoid seeing the Lake of Fire when they come there. And although God's saints will, as He said, "go out and look at the dead bodies of men who rebelled against me," it is not revealed what those dead bodies will be made of. They will certainly be observable, however, for otherwise, they would not be able to be viewed.

Brother Stuart Hiser was given a vision of this frightful scene shortly after coming to Christ. Remarkably, this was before Brother Stuart even knew it was in the Bible! Here is his testimony, in his own words:

In the early 1990s, I dreamed that I was walking in the New Jerusalem. I was walking through the city, looking at all the dwelling places there. The streets were of transparent gold throughout the city, and the buildings all were bright white. All the colors were very bright and vibrant.

The feelings while I was walking through the city were overwhelming. I felt great joy, and peace filled my whole being, but it was not just that I felt that way; it was more like

I was made of joy and peace. Everything in me was saturated with nothing but all the good and the glory of God that was around me there.

As I was walking, I came to a gate going out of the city, and then walked through the gate that led me to the outside of the city. There was green grass on both sides of the road, very pretty. As I was walking, I looked to my left, and out in the middle of the grass was a great big, transparent gold bubble. I could not see what was in the bubble. Then, all of a sudden, I had a feeling come over me of great fear and torment. It was terrifying. It consumed my whole body, and I knew – without even seeing them – that there were souls in great torment inside that bubble. Then the Spirit spoke to me and said, "You don't want to come here. Nobody wants to be here." It was terrifying. It was a year or more after this that I heard Pastor John explaining the difference between Hell and the Lake of Fire, pointing out the scriptures in Isaiah 66, and I understood then what the Lord had shown me.

I will never forget that feeling when I looked at the bubble on the outside of the gate of the New Jerusalem in that dream. The feelings from being in the city with God's glory and then the feelings of torment from being outside the city looking at the bubble were so far apart! I know that I don't want to end up inside of that bubble with all those tormented souls. I don't have words to fully describe how that really felt. It is beyond this world, both the joy and the torment.

Tophet

In time, the Valley of the Son of Hinnom (Gehenna) became notorious as a place of worship for the Ammonite god, Molech, who required child sacrifices. Multiple altars for Molech's worship had to be constructed in the valley at a place called Tophet (Jer. 7:31) in order to accommodate the multitude of Israelite parents eager to offer their children to that heathen god. Even some of the kings of Judah joined the crowds who descended into that horrible valley to burn their children to blood-thirsty gods. King Ahaz (2Chron. 28:1–3) and King Manasseh (2Chron. 33:1–6) are named specifically as visiting Tophet to sacrifice their children, but many other leaders of Israel did the same.

God sent Jeremiah to Tophet one day to prophesy against the people who worshipped there, and in the smoky haze, the Spirit cried out through the embattled prophet, "They have filled this place with the blood of innocents!" (Jer. 19:4). God angrily denounced this cruel practice of child sacrifice and swore that He would fill the Valley of the Son of Hinnom with so many Israelite bodies that it would be impossible to bury them. He said, "Behold, the days are coming when it will no longer be called Tophet or the Valley of the Son of Hinnom, but 'the Valley of Slaughter'. . . . Thus will I shatter this people and this city as one shatters a potter's vessel so that it can no longer be repaired. And they will bury in Tophet until there is no room to bury" (Jer. 7:32; 19:6, 11). God swore He would do this "because of all the evil of the children of Israel and of the children of Judah, which they have done to provoke me to anger, they, their kings, their rulers, their priests, and their prophets, and the men of Judah, and the inhabitants of Jerusalem. They have built the high places of Baal in the Valley of the Son of Hinnom to cause their sons and their daughters to pass through *the fire* for Molech, which I did not command them; neither did it enter into my heart that they should do this abomination" (Jer. 32:32, 35).

The priests and people who were there that day refused to listen to Jeremiah. "And Jeremiah came from Tophet, where the LORD had sent him to prophesy, and he stood in the court of the house of the LORD and said to all the people, 'Thus says the LORD of Hosts, the God of Israel: Behold! I am bringing against this city, and upon all its towns, the evil that I have spoken against it because they have stiffened their neck so as not to heed my words" (Jer. 19:14–15).

God's Tophet

When the Spirit proclaimed through Isaiah that "Tophet was prepared long ago" (Isa. 30:33), it was not of the Tophet in the Valley of the Son of Hinnom that the Spirit spoke, but of God's Tophet, the hideous place of everlasting fire that was created for the Devil and his angels (cf. Mt. 25:41): "Behold, the Name of the LORD[8] will come from far away, burning with his anger and a heavy burden. His lips will be full of indignation, and his tongue will be like a devouring fire. And the LORD will cause His glorious voice to be heard, and in furious anger will He cause the lowering of His arm to be seen with a consuming, cloven flame of fire, and a downpour, and hailstones. For Tophet was prepared long ago; yea, it is made ready for the King. He has made it deep; He has enlarged its fiery pyre; yea, He has provided much wood. The breath of the LORD, like a river of brimstone, has ignited it" (excerpts, Isaiah 30).

The Second Death

Another name for the Lake of Fire is "the Second Death". It is mentioned four times in the book of Revelation, and nowhere else. Here are the four places:

---

[8] "The Name of the LORD" referred to the hidden Son of God, who will come from Heaven to execute God's wrath.

Revelation 2:11

[Jesus] "He who has an ear, hear what the Spirit is saying to the Assemblies! He who overcomes will not be harmed by the Second Death."

Revelation 20:6

"Blessed and holy is he who has part in the first resurrection; over these, the Second Death has no power, but they will be priests of God and of Christ, and they will reign with him a thousand years."

Revelation 20:14

"And Death and Hell were cast into the Lake of Fire. This is the Second Death, the Lake of Fire."

Revelation 21:8

"As for the fearful, and faithless, and sinful, and filthy, and murderers, and the immoral, and sorcerers, and idolaters, and all liars, their portion will be in the lake that burns with fire and sulfur, which is the Second Death."

======

The answer to the question, "Is Gehenna another name for Hell?" is no. Gehenna is another name for the Lake of Fire, as is Tophet and the Second Death.

Chapter Three
Tartarus and the Abyss

IS TARTARUS A PLACE OF TORMENT?

Extant references to Tartarus from the ancient world are rare, but one is found in Homer's *Iliad* (8.13), written centuries before Jesus was born. There, Zeus, the Greeks' supreme god, threatened any of the gods who might dare to disobey his command: "I'll catch him and throw him down into Tartarus! A black hole that! A long way down! A Pit under the earth! Iron gates and brazen threshold! As far below Hades as Heaven is above the earth!" So, the Greeks believed that Tartarus was a place far beneath the surface of the earth.

The word *Tartarus* is used but once in the Bible, in verb form, by Peter: "God spared not the angels who sinned, but tartarized them and consigned them to chains of blackness to be held until the Day of Judgment" (2Pet. 2:4).[9] In most English translations, including the King James Version, the phrase "tartarized them" is translated as "cast them down to Hell". By and large, Christian translators have accepted as true the ancient pagan notion that Tartarus, like Hell, is somewhere below the surface of the earth. But that is not true. Tartarus is a spiritual condition; it is not a location.

Peter's teaching concerning the tartarization of angels matches that of Jude: "Angels who did not keep to their

---

[9] See Appendix, "Tartarus".

own domain, but left their proper abode,[10] God has reserved in eternal chains, under gloomy darkness, until the Judgment of the Great Day" (Jude 1:6). Nothing is said of them being tormented, just that they are bound in darkness. It is revealing that both Peter and Jude said that the fallen angels[11] are *already* "under gloomy darkness" and are *already* in "eternal chains". And there they are held, in a spiritual dungeon, until the time comes for their final judgment.

During Jesus' time on earth, the fallen angels confessed that the time for their torment was not yet come: "When Jesus had come to the other side, to the territory of the Gergesenes, two demon-possessed men met him, coming out of the tombs, so extremely fierce that no one could travel along that road. And, behold, they cried aloud, saying, 'What have we to do with you, Jesus, Son of God? Have you come here to torment us before the time?' " (Mt. 8:28–29).

======

The answer to our question, "Is Tartarus a place of torment?" is no. Tartarus is not a place at all; it is a horrible spiritual condition.

---

[10] This is apparently a reference to Genesis 6:1–2. We are told that angels *in Heaven* do not marry (Mt. 22:30; Mk. 12:25), but it appears that some of them left their heavenly bodies ("their proper abode"), came down from Heaven ("their own domain"), and possessed men so that they could mate with beautiful women (the "strange flesh" they went after – Jude 1:7). Afterward, it appears that God would not allow them to return into their angelic bodies, but condemned them to a bodiless existence, unless they could find someone or some animal to possess.

[11] See Appendix, "Fallen Angels".

WHO IS TARTARUS FOR?

Peter's mention of tartarized angels is in a chapter that is not about angels at all (2Pet. 2); it is instead devoted to warning God's children to be faithful, lest God tartarize *them*! God's tartarization of some of His angels is but one illustration among several that Peter used to demonstrate how severely God deals with treachery in His kingdom.

It is significant that Peter said nothing about sinners being tartarized. This is because only those who have received the Spirit of God and been born anew into God's family can be, as Jude put it, "twice dead and uprooted" (Jude 1:12). All who are now in Christ were once dead in sin (cf. Eph. 2:1, 5; Col. 2:13), but when God tartarizes a believer, that believer is made dead in sin again, but this time permanently. Solomon warned God's people in the Old Testament, "A man who, being often reproved, stiffens his neck shall suddenly be broken, and that without remedy" (Prov. 29:1). Tartarization, then, is a curse reserved for self-willed, treacherous servants of God, whether heavenly beings or men. On earth during the Old Testament, that meant treacherous against the law of Moses, but in this covenant, it means treacherous against the Son of God, of whom that law spoke.

In their comments on the subject, both Peter and Jude focused on tartarized believers who act as leaders among God's people, but God has also tartarized some who are not leaders, such as those in Israel who mocked God's call for repentance: "The LORD of Hosts called for weeping, and for mourning, and for baldness,[12] and for the girding on of sackcloth. But, behold, joy and gladness, killing oxen and slaughtering sheep, eating flesh and drinking

---

[12] That is, for heads to be shaved as a sign of contrition.

wine, saying, 'Let us eat and drink, for tomorrow we will die!' And in my hearing, it was revealed by the LORD of Hosts, 'Atonement for this iniquity will never be made for *y*ou until *y*ou die!'" (Isa. 22:12–14). Likewise, Jesus warned all his fellow Israelites, those who followed him as well as his enemies, that whoever blasphemes the holy Spirit will never be forgiven, "either in this present world or in the one to come" (Mt. 12:32). Such blasphemers are damned while they live, cursed to live out the rest of their lives in sin with no hope of forgiveness.

======

The answer to our question, "Who is Tartarus for?" is that it is for treacherous members of the kingdom of God.

IF TARTARUS IS NOT A PLACE, THEN WHERE ARE TARTARIZED BELIEVERS?

Peter revealed the answer to this question when he warned the saints that they would be "among *y*ou" (2Pet. 2:1), being "preserved under punishment until the Day of Judgment" (2Pet. 2:9). They are children of God, but they are cursed with spiritual blindness and, so, continue worshipping with the body of Christ without realizing they have no hope of eternal life (cf. 2Pet. 2:13).

======

The answer to our question, "Where are tartarized believers?" is that they are among believers, living and worshipping with them.

CAN SOMEONE IN TARTARUS REPENT?

No one, of himself, is capable of godly sorrow for sin, for repentance is the work of God within a heart. Jesus told a group of his fellow Jews, "No one can come to me unless the Father who sent me draw him" (Jn. 6:44). The earliest believers understood this, and when the believing Jews in Jerusalem heard that some Gentiles had received the Spirit, they rejoiced – not because those Gentiles had decided they would repent and believe the gospel, but because God had "granted repentance" to them (Acts 11:18). In Tartarus, however, no soul is ever granted the godly sorrow that produces repentance. Such is the spiritual condition of Satan, as described by God Himself: "His heart is hard, like a stone. Yea, it is hard like a lower millstone" (Job 41:24). And it is God who hardened it so; that is tartarization.

God grants no repentance to those in Hell, either, but the great difference between Hell and Tartarus, and the element which makes Tartarus far worse, is that a tartarized soul is *condemned to stay alive* in their sinful condition, without hope of forgiveness because forgiveness follows repentance, and God will not grant it. Those in Hell cannot add sin to their record and make their final judgment worse, but for souls in Tartarus, just the opposite is true. They are cursed to continue to live according to their own will until God allows them to die. As Peter said, they are cursed children of God who cannot cease from sin. They are continually making their final judgment worse. For souls in Tartarus, to be in Hell, where they could do nothing, would be a blessing.

Judas the betrayer discerned that he would never be forgiven for what he had done. He was with Jesus at the Last Supper, perhaps looking into Jesus' eyes, when the Lord said, "Woe to that man by whom the Son of man is betrayed! It were good for him if that man had not been born" (Mt. 26:24). And later that same night, after betray-

ing Jesus, rather than continue living out what he knew
was now a damned life, Judas killed himself – and awful
as that was, suicide was for him the best option. If anything is surprising about Judas' suicide, it is that God even
allowed him to do it.

The beauty and goodness of life on earth is that it is a
place of almost boundless hope, a place of opportunity to
do what is good in God's sight, a place of opportunity for
growth in understanding and righteousness, a place where
we may be corrected and may change, a place where
choices are still available and responses can still be made
to God's love. For tartarized believers, however, that no
longer holds true.

======

The answer to our question, "Can someone in Tartarus
repent?" is no; God will not allow it.

DO TARTARIZED PEOPLE KNOW THEY ARE TARTARIZED?

Referring to tartarized people, Peter made the following comments: "They are spots and blemishes . . . reveling
in their deceitful ways while they feast with you. . . . For
if after escaping the defilements of the world through the
knowledge of the Lord and Savior, Jesus Christ, they are
again entangled in them and overcome, their last state is
worse than the first. It would be better for them not to
have known the way of righteousness than, after knowing
it, to turn from the holy commandment delivered to them"
(Excerpts, 2Peter 2).

This description of tartarized souls leaves no doubt
that tartarized children of God are blind to their condition
and that they feel that they belong among the saints; in-

deed, they may even feel qualified to lead them. If they understood their true spiritual condition, they could not possibly "revel" and "feast" with the saints, as Peter said they do. They are the "impostors" whom Paul said would come, "deceiving and being deceived" (2Tim. 3:13).

That those in Tartarus do not know they are there is one element which makes Tartarus the most horrific of all spiritual conditions. The tartarized leaders of Israel certainly did not realize how wretched their spiritual condition was: "Strangers consume his strength, but he does not know it; yea, gray hair is showing up on him, but he does not know it. The pride of Israel shows on his face, but they do not return to the LORD their God, nor seek Him in all this" (Hos. 7:9–10). Tartarized leaders among the saints in this covenant are like them.

Swift Destruction?

For years before I understood tartarization, I wondered how Peter could have said that "swift destruction" would come upon false teachers in the body of Christ and that "their destruction is not asleep," inasmuch as he also said that those false teachers would enjoy successful religious careers. Tartarization is the answer; that is the "swift destruction" which comes upon those who stubbornly refuse to obey the truth God has shown them. It is a destruction so full of wrath that God will not even let them know it is happening, and so, they unwittingly, confidently continue in their damned state.

Concerning the tartarized believers who become ministers, Peter gave this warning to the saints: "There will be false teachers among *you*, who will introduce opinions that lead to damnation. . . . These, like unreasoning beasts of nature, . . . speak evil of things they do not understand . . . . They cannot cease from sin, and they seduce unstable souls. They are cursed children [of God], having forsaken the right way and gone astray in following the way of Balaam, who loved the reward of unrighteousness[13]. . . . They are wells without water, clouds driven by a storm,[14] for whom is reserved the blackness of eternal darkness. . . . Making pretentious, vain speeches [sermons], they entice to sensuality through lusts of the flesh those who once had truly escaped from those who live in error, promising them liberty, themselves being servants of corruption" (excerpts, 2Peter 2).

Tartarized believers are among the third kind of soil in Jesus' parable of the Four Kinds of Soil (Mt. 13:3–8, 18–23). According to that parable, the first kind of soil rejected the truth because of ungodly influences; the second kind of soil turned away because of persecution; but the third kind of soil failed because of the deceitfulness of riches and desire for worldly things. Those of this kind of soil do not cease worshipping with the saints, and they may think they are doing well, but their spiritual growth has been stopped and they bear no fruit acceptable to God. As Peter said, they continue "feasting" with the saints, though they are "spots and blemishes" on the fabric of the congregation's fellowship. Indeed, they may even become leaders of the congregation, delivering impressive sermons which attract men's souls (cf. 2Pet. 2:1, 18–19). And in the end, when Jesus rejects them, they will be very surprised (cf. Mt. 7:21–23).

The misguided confidence of such believers is a most fearsome curse. Under this curse, some of these doomed

---

[13] See Appendix, "The Way of Balaam".

[14] A reference to Proverbs 25:14: "A man who boasts of a false gift is like clouds and wind without rain."

souls even claim to be apostles of Jesus (2Cor. 11:13). They light their own fire, Isaiah said, setting others on fire with their doctrines, who in turn become little sparks reflective of their leader, and those sparks pass along to others their vain form of service to God (Isa. 50:11). Under this curse, tartarized leaders of Israel spent fortunes evangelizing others (Mt. 23:15). Under this curse, God's own servants are transformed into ministers of Satan (2Cor. 11:15), with a heart as hard as Satan's. These ministers proclaim a gospel that contradicts the truth, and they may even persecute the upright, "thinking they are offering a service to God" (Jn. 16:2). It is because of them, Peter said, that "the way of truth will be spoken evil of" (2Pet. 2:2).

Paul taught that God is just, to turn over to darkness those who have been given the light of His Son but who then refuse to walk in it. Said Paul, "Because they did not receive the love of the truth, God will send them a strong delusion," causing these formerly loved sons and daughters to "believe the lie, so that they all might be damned who did not believe the truth, but took pleasure in unrighteousness" (2Thess. 2:10–12). And before he came to earth, Christ prayed for God to likewise blind those in Israel who would reject him as their Messiah: "Return, O LORD, a recompense upon them according to the work of their hands. Give them hardness of heart, your curse upon them. In your anger, pursue and destroy them from under the heavens of the LORD!" (Lam. 3:64–66).

Blessed and Used by God

When God blesses tartarized saints, it is only to blind them to their true spiritual condition and make them bold in their error. Such children of God often have a sense that God is using them, and they are correct in that, but they do not realize that God is using them only to try the hearts of His other children who still have hope. My father drifted away from God once, yet continued in his ministry. Sinners would be convicted by his preaching, he told us, and would fall to their knees and weep for their sins. Then he added, "They looked up to me as a holy man, but I would have given anything to be as free in spirit as they were." Thankfully, he was not tartarized; God allowed him to feel his need of forgiveness, and he repented and was forgiven. For those who are not granted repentance, however, Jesus described what their plea will be in the end when they are condemned: "Not everyone who says to me, 'Lord! Lord!' will enter into the kingdom of heaven, but he who does the will of my Father who is in heaven. Many will say to me in that day, 'Lord! Lord! Haven't we prophesied in your name, and cast out demons in your name, and performed many miracles in your name?'" (Mt. 7:21–23). It is sobering to consider that even after being tartarized, these cursed children of God were still able to use their blessings, including spiritual gifts, to minister to others. It is admittedly difficult to imagine a cursed child of God still healing the sick, prophesying, rejoicing in the Spirit, etc. But that is our own way of thinking. Jesus said it would happen with some of God's children. Too late, though, those children will learn that God has only been using them, even in their damned state, for others' good.

We cannot help but see the harshness of this; at the same time, it is true. And it is a truth which makes every wise soul tremble. God's judgments against sin can be extremely harsh. But whatever God decides to do with anyone is perfectly just because God is perfect and just.

A Mixture

Although souls in Tartarus still have choices and are free to make changes, no choice or change they make can please God, regardless of how good those choices appear to men. Jesus warned his disciples, "That which is highly esteemed among men is an abomination in the sight of God" (Lk. 16:15), and so it is with tartarized ministers. They may be highly esteemed by thousands, but they are ministering in spiritual blindness, leading the blind toward the deepest ditch of all.

God hates wickedness, of course, but He hates a mixture of wickedness and goodness even more. There was a pastor in Laodicea whose love for God was mixed with love for the world. Jesus said to him, "I know your works, that you are neither cold nor hot. I would that you were either cold or hot. So, because you are lukewarm, and neither hot nor cold, I am about to vomit you out of my mouth" (Rev. 3:15–16). "Mixed" is an apt description of Tartarus, for it is a mixture of blessings with the greatest curse, a mixture of life and death. Their souls are blessed with life, but are cursed with the kind of life they must live. They are blessed with the ability to change, but they can only change from one sinful thing to another. They can still grow (they have no choice about that), but they can only grow more damned – and this, they constantly do.

Paul described such believers as abandoned by Christ, being "reprobate concerning the faith" (2Tim. 3:8; cf. 2Cor. 13:5). Of such believers, Jeremiah said, "Men will call them 'rejected silver', for the LORD has rejected them" (Jer. 6:30). That is a tragic end to a life once sanctified by the Spirit of God; yet, heartbreaking as it is, we must confess that it really happens. To deny that it happens is unwise, and it changes nothing.

======

The answer to our question, "Do tartarized people know they are tartarized?" is no.

CAN WE KNOW WHO HAS BEEN TARTARIZED?

God is incomparably merciful and very slow to anger. He has joyfully welcomed home many a believer who drifted away from righteousness and wanted to come back to Him. Jesus' parables of the Prodigal Son (Lk. 15:11–32) and the Ninety and Nine (Mt. 18:12–13) powerfully show this to be true. James spoke of backslidden believers being restored in faith: "Brothers, if anyone among *y*ou is led astray from the truth and someone turns him back, let him know that he who turns the sinner from his wandering way will save a soul from death and will cover a multitude of sins" (Jas. 5:19–20). Jesus said, "There is joy among God's angels over one sinner who repents" (Lk. 15:10), but that is only because the angels follow God's lead. If He were not rejoicing over that repentant soul, the angels certainly would not. Heartfelt repentance is a gift from God (cf. Acts 11:19), and it makes God happy for one of His beloved, backslidden children to receive that gift.

But how do we know (1) who has fallen away, since tartarized believers continue to be religious, and (2) who will God still allow to repent, and who will He not? The answer is that, as Jesus told his disciples, "With men, it is impossible." God alone knows where each soul stands with Him. He does, in many cases, reveal to His servants the spiritual condition of others, but apart from such revelation, it is impossible for us to discern between a back-slidden soul whom He will still allow to repent and a tartarized soul whom He has rejected.

Paul wrote to Timothy concerning two men, Hymenaeus and Alexander, who had ruined their good conscience and "made shipwreck of their faith" (1Tim. 1:19). Moreover, he said, they had begun teaching a doctrine that was so detrimental to the saints that Paul had "turned them over to Satan" (1Tim. 1:20). But Paul seemed to have a healing purpose for doing so! He told Timothy that he had turned Hymenaeus and Alexander over to Satan, "that they may be taught not to blaspheme." In other words, those two foolish believers might still learn to do right. The lesson in Paul's words is clear: judge no one, but wait on the judgment of God. God has children who have done some wicked deeds; still, no one is hopeless unless God says so.

Hymenaeus and Alexander may or may not have learned their lesson and repented; we are not told. I hope they did, but even if they did not, it does not mean they were tartarized. There are believers who die without repenting, though they could have. Paul speaks of some Corinthian believers who did that (1Cor. 11:29–30). But he then adds that God judged those believers with death so that they would not be condemned with the world (1Cor. 11:32). So, it is possible to die without repenting of something with which God is displeased, and yet still have hope.[15] To die that way is sad, certainly, but a harsh chastisement meant to punish and to save is not nearly as bad as being cursed to live a life that is damned. For someone

---

[15] Examples of this may be Ananias and Sapphira, whom God killed for lying to Peter (Acts 5:1–11). If a premature death was the only punishment for their error, they were blessed, compared to being cursed by God to live on among His saints in a damned state.

in that state, John said not to waste your breath by praying for him: "If anyone sees his brother committing a sin that does not call for death, he shall ask [God], and He will give him life for those who commit sins that do not call for death. There is a sin that calls for death; I do not say that he should pray for that. All unrighteousness is sin, but there is a sin that does not call for death" (1Jn. 5:16–17). And again, only Jesus knows who has committed which kind of sin – Jesus and those to whom he chooses to reveal it.

======

The answer to the question, "Can we know who has been tartarized?" is no – unless God chooses to reveal it to us.

WHAT IS THE ABYSS?

Except for the mysteries of Babylon (Rev. 17:5) and Tartarus, the Abyss may be the least understood of all the dwelling places for evil mentioned in the Bible. Any very deep place may be called an abyss, such as the depths of the sea (e.g., Gen. 1:2; Ex. 15:5, 8), or even Hell itself (Rom. 10:7), since it is deep in the heart of the earth. But the Abyss of Revelation is neither of those two. It is to that Abyss that the demons begged Jesus not to send them when he was about to cast them out of a man (Lk. 8:31), which tells us that the Abyss of Revelation is a dreadful place.

Nothing is said about the Abyss in book of Revelation until the ninth chapter, and it is mentioned six times after that, playing a significant role in end-time events. The first time John mentions the Abyss, he tells us that a "star" (an angel) fell from Heaven "and the key to the shaft of the Abyss was given to him. And he opened the shaft of the Abyss, and smoke came up out of the shaft like the smoke of a burning furnace, and the sun and the air were darkened with the smoke from the shaft. And then, out of the smoke came locusts to the earth, and power was given to them like the power that scorpions of the earth have. And it was given to them not to kill but to torture [those who do not have the seal of God] five months, and their torment was like the torment of a scorpion when it stings a man. And in those days, men will seek death and will by no means find it, and they will long to die, but death will flee from them. The locusts have as king over them the angel of the Abyss. His name in Hebrew is 'Abaddon', but his name in Greek is 'Apollyon' " (excerpts, Revelation 9).[16]

Where did these bizarre creatures come from? Could they have lived on earth at a previous time and been imprisoned in the Abyss to be released at the end time to serve God's purposes? Or did God create them from the smoke that arose from the newly opened Abyss? We are given no answers. They are mentioned here for the first and last time in Scripture. Fortunately, however, John was granted some information about the Abyss itself.

In Revelation 11:7, John makes a comment, almost as an aside, that is striking. In the course of telling about God's unnamed Two Witnesses who will come and prophesy in Jerusalem before the end of the age, John informs us that these two holy men will be slain by "the Beast that

---

[16] Apollyon, or "Destroyer", the king over the creatures from the Abyss, appears to be a fallen angel with great authority (cf. Rev. 20:1), one of the most powerful of the "stars" drawn down to earth by the tail of the Dragon (Rev. 12:4). In the Old Testament, Apollyon is the angel who passed over Egypt to kill all the firstborn of the Egyptians (Ex. 12:23), and he is also mentioned elsewhere (Job 26:6; 28:22; Prov. 15:11).

ascends from the Abyss." This, by itself, does not shed great light on the Abyss, but when other information about the Beast is added, what we learn is astonishing.

First, the Beast is a man; he is not a beast as we typically use the word. John also indicates that the Beast is human by telling us the Beast came up "out of the sea" (Rev. 13:1), the sea representing peoples of earth (Rev. 17:15). The Beast is supernaturally intelligent (Ezek. 28:3–5; Dan. 8:23–24), and this will not be his first experience of earthly existence. By the time he appears near the end of this age, he will have already reigned as a king at some point in history (Rev. 17:8). Moreover, in his heart, the Beast harbors the same virulent hatred for Jews that Satan does. In fact, he is in such harmony with Satan that when he is released from the Abyss to reign on earth again, Satan will give the Beast "his power, and his throne, and great authority" (Rev. 13:2). The Beast is so intent on accomplishing his evil purposes, especially his goal of exterminating the Jews, that his passion consumes him. He cares nothing at all for women or family life (Dan. 11:37). He is Satan's all-time favorite person, his most reliable tool.

Whoever the Beast is, his first kingship did not come to an end because he died, though history books may say that he did.[17] Rather, he was taken from this life and imprisoned in the Abyss, to be held there until God's appointed time for him to return to reign again on earth.

And lastly, we are told that Satan will be imprisoned in the Abyss[18] during the thousand-year reign of Jesus on

---

[17] See Appendix, "The Beast".

[18] Hell (1Pet. 3:19) and the Abyss (Rev. 20:7) are both referred to as prisons.

earth, and then brought out to deceive the nations again for a season (Rev. 20:7).

======

So the answer to the question, "What is the Abyss?" is that, based upon the information given to us in Revelation, it appears to be a holding pen for especially destructive and wicked beings. The Beast is imprisoned in the Abyss for a time before being brought out again to fulfill God's preordained course for him, and Satan is imprisoned there during the thousand-year reign of Jesus on earth, before being brought out of the Abyss for a season (Rev. 20:7).[19]

WHERE IS THE ABYSS AND WHAT ARE THE CONDITIONS IN IT?

John said that when Satan was seized by God's angel in Revelation 20:2–3, that powerful angel cast Satan "into the Abyss", not "down into" it. It was the same with the fallen angels who were tartarized. Peter did not tell us that they were "cast down" into Tartarus. The Abyss cannot be in Heaven because the angels who opened the Abyss had to come down from Heaven to open it (Rev. 9:1; 20:1). Furthermore, smoke "arose" and the Beast "ascended" out of the Abyss. So, it appears that the Abyss is somehow positioned downward from Heaven, but not necessarily below the surface of the earth. It would surprise me if it were not in some way connected with the earth's underworld, but the Abyss is a unique kind of spiritual prison that could be hidden by God somewhere else.

---

[19] It was noticing that God re-used both Satan and the Beast after they had spent time in the Abyss, which caused me to wonder earlier if the dreadfully equipped locusts that Apollyon released from the Abyss had previously lived on the earth.

Other than the demons pleading with Jesus not to cast them into the Abyss, we are given no clues as to the conditions within the Abyss. What exactly they were thinking when they begged not to be cast in there is unknown.

======

The answer to the question, "Where is the Abyss?" is that its location is not revealed. We are only told that it is downward from heaven. The answer to the questions, "What are the conditions in it? is that the conditions in it are unknown, but we do know that demons do not want to be in there.

Chapter Four
Responses to the Study on Hell

Bro. John,

Thank you! I am so grateful that I had the opportunity to proofread your study on *What the Bible Really Says about Hell*. What a wonderful experience I found in the pages of your study!

First of all, as I read in the beginning how you and the boys began your study, I was not expecting to find a "pause" page that so tenderly spoke of the Father and the Son and the "innocent pain" that they both endured so that we could be where we are today. My! "Innocent pain." I had never thought of pain in that way, but that is exactly what it was – innocent. Considering the innocent pain they both endured touched me deeply. I felt the love of God as I read it.

As I continued reading, I found myself not so much "engulfed in the flames" of Hell as I was overwhelmed by the love of God in everything I was reading. I realized that this was not just a study on Hell, but a wonderful story of God, God's love, God's power, God's righteousness, God's justice, God's patience, God's long-suffering towards mankind – just plain "God". God is right; God is fair; God is just; God is all-powerful; God's power can destroy or save. I found myself several times stopping and asking myself, "Do you believe what you are reading?" I knew that if I did, it would compel me to live God's way, wanting only His desires in my heart.

After I completed the reading, I sat here soaking in what I had just read. It was a story of God the Creator.

He is the only One with power to "take and destroy" or "save and restore". And this side of the grave is the only place we can live according to God's will. After death, all is said and done. Nothing else can be accomplished. As Brother Darren's song says: *"How should we live, knowing the soul never dies?"*

Thank you for this story of God.

Sandy

===

Brother John,

When you were speaking tonight about Tartarus and what the darkness of no conviction for doing evil must be like, I was reminded of something Peter wrote which helps me see what you were saying about the "tartarized" condition of the fallen angels (1Pet. 1:12): "To [the prophets], it was revealed that they were ministering those things not to themselves but to *you*, which things are now reported to *you* by those who preach the gospel to *you* by the holy Spirit sent from Heaven, into which things angels long to look." This shows us that angels (both fallen and faithful) desire to look into the light which we can have in Jesus. This was something God knew beforehand, that even faithful angels would have the desire, but not the grace, to understand the gospel and the way of the Spirit.

Jude referred only to fallen angels when he wrote, "Angels who did not keep to their own domain but left their proper abode, [God] has reserved in eternal chains, under gloomy darkness, until the Judgment of the Great Day" (v. 6). However, even though they are "reserved in chains under darkness", they still have a desire to dwell among the saints. If that were not the case, then why would there be evil spirits hiding amongst us, as we have found out in recent times? They certainly have a desire to be around us. Satan, especially, remembers what it was like to be in the presence of God. He envied and wanted God's glory while he was there in Heaven with God, and he envies God's glory in us now, and likes to be around it. Yet, he and his angels have lost the opportunity to be blessed in any way by what they see in us. Their desire proceeds from an evil heart. In the "Tartarus" condition, nothing produces in them conviction for evildoing – not even the holiest of things that they might witness among the saints. It must bring an even greater condemnation upon them to see the wonderful blessings from God upon the body of Christ on earth.

Paul said that apostles "are made a spectacle (Greek *theatron*) before the world, to both angels and men." It appears that God intended from the beginning for men and angels to watch us who have the Spirit, so that in the working out of our salvation, there may be a blessing for upright angels and men, and greater condemnation for ungodly angels and men.

That verse from Jude does not say that God took away the desire of fallen angels to look into the things we have, but when they "left their proper abode", they lost the opportunity for that desire to lead to any blessing for them. Cast down now into this state of darkness and "chained" to it, they are condemned to become more and more guilty by whatever holy things they witness, but from which they are forever barred. They just can't stop themselves from making it ever worse for themselves in the Final Judgment.

I hope we can live so that we do not disappoint the faithful angels who are watching us, hoping to learn more about their God, if God enables them. We can learn the fear of God from many places, and if we carefully consid-

er these things, we will learn from the example of the wretched angels who followed Satan and were, with him, cast out of Heaven into that place called "Tartarus".
Damien

======

Yes, Damien!

And your comments reminded me of what Paul said that faithful saints are now doing, that is, educating spiritual powers in Heaven concerning the things of God: ". . . so that through the Assembly of God, the multi-faceted wisdom of God might now be made known to the rulers and authorities among heavenly beings."
Pastor John

==

Dear Brother John,

Last night was so good for me to be able to be with you all to learn about the "abode of the dead", or Hell (and other places). Reading the handout again this morning, I was very thankful to have been there to hear the truths that were talked about. I would love to pass it on to others.

Some things that stood out and some thoughts I had were:

All who are on the earth are before the Lord, and all who are in Hell are before the Lord. There is no escape from Him in either place.

All those who are in Hell know that truth. I have been thinking this morning that only on earth can a wicked person believe that there is an escape from Hell and, so, receive a type of "rest" (from the fear of God). In that way only, in believing a lie, is there a sort of rest for the wicked in this life.

I loved learning that Job knew that descending into Hell was a permanent condition, but he still had hope that God would not forsake him. He knew something about what was to come in his prayer written in Job 14:13: "O that you would hide me away in [Hell] and conceal me until your anger is passed, that you would appoint me a time and remember me!" He was looking for the appearing of Jesus while he lived, just as we do now. We also are "looking for that blessed hope and the glorious appearing of the great God and our Savior Jesus Christ" (Tit. 2:13).

Then, hearing how Jesus did remember those held in Paradise was so good. He rescued the righteous. He didn't forget those who trusted in him. And now for those who belong to him through the Spirit, he does not delay or withhold himself when this life is over. There is no waiting anymore.

I also loved learning that God had organization in Hell and that the righteous were separated from the wicked. That was merciful and kind. And now, even for those who waited, the discomfort they felt is at an end.

There are still things that are going around in my head from last night. It was so good. Thank you.

Danny M.

======================================

Brother John,

I understood tonight that Hell was not created for man, but for the Devil and his angels. Does this mean that the Devil and his angels sinned before Adam and Eve?

Randell

======

Hi Brother Randell,

You misunderstood me; I am sorry that I did not make that clearer. Matthew 25:41 does tell us that there is a fire prepared for the Devil and his angels (rather than for men, we assume). But which fire is that? Is it Hell or the Lake of Fire? I think the evidence points to the latter. So, it is Gehenna, not Hell, that was made for the Devil and his angels.

But as to your question, yes, the Devil sinned before Adam and Eve did. He is the first liar. That is why Jesus called him "the father of lies" (Jn. 8:44b). He either inspired the serpent that lied to Eve in the Garden of Eden, or he was the lying serpent himself (cf. Rev. 12:9). As for the angels that followed the Devil in his wickedness, I suppose that they fell into sin shortly after the Devil fell, but the Bible does not give us a time frame for that.

Pastor John

===

Hi, John.

This evening I began to read through your Hell study again, and as I got to the "Can Anyone Escape Hell" section, I started to have some feelings, and I began to drift into them. You were talking about men of the Old Testament having faith to believe that God would deliver them from [the Paradise portion of Hell], and then having Jesus actually come and deliver them from it, and a feeling of appreciation flooded me. It all depended on Jesus!

I laid the study down on my chest and let gratitude fill me. I thanked God for many things, for Jesus especially, that He has made my heart open to the truth and that He has made my life perfect for me – just because He loves me. He, because it pleased Him, has given me understanding in Him and a love for truth that many "mighty" earthly men do not have. He has kept me, preserved me, and has created circumstances throughout life that have thus far kept the lust of the flesh, or the pride of life, or any other weakness or sin from sweeping me away. He has given me a holy Spirit that has the power and the love that will keep me from that place I am reading about – Hell. He paid the price. He did it all. These were some of my thoughts when I stopped reading – I just wanted to give glory to Him.

OK, then I picked the book back up and flipped back to the page where I read, "Let's Pause a Minute to Honor God"!!!! Wow! It goes on: "We are loved by God! . . . We must avoid the pitfall of pride, lest our study become merely academic. . . . We have hope of eternal life because of the willingness of both the Son *and* the Father to suffer. . . . So, give praise and honor to both the Father and the Son for the pain they endured to bring about so great a salvation," etc.

It sure was a wonderful feeling to have already done those things when I read it. To be exhorted to do the very thing God had just put in my heart to do, did something in me! That was God putting it in my heart to give Him glory, for He knew what was on the next page! I love His ways and His feelings.

One would think that a book about Hell would primarily leave us with negative feelings of dread or fear, but I found just the opposite to be true. Throughout the book, I kept feeling the love of God, both opening the truth about that place (vs. myth and fiction), and in sending us His Son Jesus so that we don't have to go there. To me, this book was as much about the love of God for us as it was about Hell itself.

I'm enjoying the book very much. But I really wanted to pause and testify to my experience.

Good night and thank you for your labor.

Gary

======

Hi, Gary.

If after reading the book, you feel like offering humble praise to God, then you got the point.

Pastor John

==

Daddy,

I take it that the Devil and his angels sinned before Adam and Eve, but were not cast out of Heaven until Jesus rose from the dead and ascended into Heaven. I wonder if God even pointed the Devil out in Heaven as "a bad guy", or if He kept all of it in His heart, letting him deceive those he could among the angels until they were all suddenly gone. . . . Is there any evidence one way or another?

te.

======

Hi, Token.

God never told anyone Satan was evil while he and his angels were in Heaven. All those thousands of years, un-known to anyone, God was using Satan to try the hearts of other heavenly creatures, and that continued until Jesus ascended and was glorified. Then, Michael and his angels fought with Satan and his angels and finally cast them out (Rev. 12:7–9).

Evil spirits were still in Heaven during the Old Testament. In 1Kings 22, God and an evil spirit spoke quite openly with one another in a heavenly counsel before He sent that spirit to earth to be a lying spirit in the mouths of Israel's false prophets. But who among the heavenly host knew that spirit was evil? I think no one did, except the Father and His hidden Son. Many faithful creatures in Heaven must have felt awkward around Satan and the angels under him, but when they saw God do nothing about it, what could they have thought, and what could they have done?

You will remember also that Jesus tolerated Judas in silence for years, keeping the other disciples in the dark about him. Indeed, even up to the moment Judas exposed himself as the betrayer by leading the mob to arrest Jesus in Gethsemane, the other disciples (with the possible exception of John) thought that Judas was a disciple in good standing. Just so, up to the moment Satan was cast out, many in Heaven may have assumed that he was as he appeared to be: a faithful servant of God, whom God chose to carry out some very important missions (e.g., the affliction of Job, the Temptation of Jesus, etc.)

Daddy

==

John,

There are many thoughts that arise from last night. Kay and I had a good time this morning discussing it and reading some verses from the Bible.

We read Romans 9:14–23. In particular, these verses stood out (22–23): "So what, if God, desiring to demonstrate His wrath and to make known His power, bore with great patience the vessels of wrath made for destruction, so that He might also make known the riches of His glory upon the vessels of mercy that He prepared beforehand for glory."

"Fitted to destruction" reminded me of Peter's statement, "These, like unreasoning beasts of nature, *were* born to be caught and killed." That is an amazing statement, now that we have more understanding of it. Those "vessels of wrath" are not merely endured with long-suffering but with *much* long-suffering. Paul is saying that God is showing His wrath and making His power known, but to whom? Surely to those who are being blessed the way Romans 9:23 describes. As much as the Flood and Sodom and Gomorrah are examples to us, so it is when we see someone in this state. I expect that we will see more of it in the future. God wants us to understand it now.

This was the same passage (the one from Romans) that I was considering when the Lord posed two questions to me: (1) "If I told you that no matter what you did, you would not be saved, then what would you do?" (This question came with the feeling that I would retain the knowledge of God that I had), and (2) "If I showed you a way to be saved, then what would you do?"

I now know the first question was describing the state, or close to it, of being "tartarized" – utterly helpless and unable to do anything that counted as right before God (everything wrong in His eyes).

Kay and I also discussed the fact that for a long time, Satan and demons, as angels in Heaven, were able to come before God and hear God and even receive instruction in what to do. We wondered about the many ministers of Christianity who do hear from God. A "tartarized" person may still be allowed into the presence of God and truly hear from God, and yet it is all damning them the more certainly. It seems to me that Christianity itself must be connected to this casting into Tartarus in some way. The rejection of light by early believers was rewarded by God with the darkness of Christianity, but still God has a time yet reserved for His people to get out of it before it is cast into that inescapable place when God sends the "strong delusion".

The way into Tartarus is to refuse to repent. If that is your heart's wish, then God will grant it. Getting into Tartarus may be more a process than an instantaneous thing. The mercy of God may just make it that way because "when He makes a way to His wrath" there is no escape.

Paul, Peter, John and Jude wrote letters which show that they saw the rising up of this unrepentant spirit. They marveled at it and warned those who could hear them. Clearly, Peter and Jude discerned in the Spirit that some among believers had been abandoned by God. We live in a time when God is revealing truth to us, and it must surely come to pass that this truth will be widely known and taught. The more we have from God, the more is expected of us, and the greater the possible punishments for rejection. These are clear principles in God.

This is wonderful, but so fearful.

Damien

==

John,

Damien wrote, "The way into Tartarus is to refuse to repent. If that is your heart's wish, then God will grant it."

Wow, John, this was a good insight by Damien. What a thought!

When we refuse to repent, it seems that non-repentance is what our heart really wants, and one day, God will give us our heart's desire – just as He said. He

will give us a place to live eternally where we will not, and cannot, repent – and all the misery that goes with it.
Gary

======

Hi, Gary.

I am glad you pointed out to me that comment from Damien. Tartarized souls cannot refuse to repent, of course, because God does not grant repentance to them, but refusing to repent while the door is still open is certainly the way into that awful state.
Pastor John

==

Hey,

Damien wrote, "The way into Tartarus is to refuse to repent. If that is your heart's wish, then God will grant it. Getting into Tartarus may be more a process than an instantaneous thing."

Does that mean that one can be in a half-tartarized state?
te.

======

No. It's all or nothing. Either it is hopeless (Tartarus) or there is hope. That said, it is normal that, as with anything else, whether a blessing or a curse, a person backslides slowly, by degrees of stubborn disobedience and dullness of heart, until he provokes God to curse him to that degree.
Daddy

==

Hi,

I loved what you taught us last night about being "tartarized". It put more fear of God in me than ever, but at the same time, it gives me more encouragement than ever.

It makes me want to obey God more than ever. And it feels cleaner than ever. I love that.

During the night, I kept having thoughts about the word "adulterous". The first was that a person can be physically close to their spouse, but if they have physically been with someone else, or if in their heart they are not with their spouse, that is adulterous. Then I remembered how Jesus defined adultery, that even if a man looked at and lusted after a woman, he had already committed adultery in his heart. I was also remembering what we read last night in the Tartarus study, how it is better to be one way or the other, hot or cold, and that being "mixed" is worse than all. Then, I was having thoughts of the Great Whore in Revelation, Christianity. She is not even married. She is not in covenant with God, but she loves the physical act. Christianity loves the physical act of worshipping God. But that's all that they have; it is just of the flesh. And then, how God is calling His children to "come out of her, my people, that *you* be not partakers of her sins, and that *you* receive not of her plagues."

It all goes back to the heart! That's just what we hear God saying to His people through the prophets. I don't know quite how to put it all together, but it feels like I am learning something.

Donna

======

Hi, Sister Donna.

Yes, it does feel as if you are learning something.

I would not at all say that the children of God who are still inside Christianity have nothing but the ceremonial forms of the Christian religion with which to worship. After all, to be a child of God means to have the Spirit within, by which one can really worship God. But I must say that, being in Christianity, their worship is "mixed", which to God has always been anathema. I think that God would rather His children either be nothing but Christians or be completely separated from that abomination ("Come out of her!"). It is God's children trying to force a mixture of His holy Spirit with the Great Whore's wicked spirit that causes most of the confusion and division that exists among the saints on earth today. May God save us from that great error!

Pastor John

==

John,

I have a question. If a person has been "tartarized", the way I understand it, there is no coming back. But when I think of King Nebuchadnezzar eating grass seven years, would that be an example of reversal?

Wendell

=======

Hi, Wendell.

Since last night, that question has been asked of me a couple of times.

You were right with your first thought, Wendell. There is no coming back from Tartarus. God doesn't play around with people's souls. He is eternally serious about every judgment He makes. No one in Tartarus can possibly return to the good life where God speaks to man and guides him toward righteousness.

King Nebuchadnezzar was not tartarized by God when he was given the mind of an animal. I say that with confidence because it is obvious that with the mind of an animal, out in the field eating grass, Nebuchadnezzar could not have been sinning at all, just as animals do not sin. Much less was the king sinning constantly, as those in Tartarus are condemned to do.

God is very patient and slow to anger, and He chastens whom He loves because in chastening, there is hope. He will work with us for years to overcome a fault, but He is nobody's fool. He can be provoked to wrath, and the greatest wrath falls upon those who harden their hearts repeatedly against the grace of God, and He ceases to chasten them, thereby consigning them to Tartarus.

Anyone who claims that he has been to Tartarus and back is either ignorant or trying to impress people with an extraordinary tale and false humility. Or, it could possibly be that he is under the wicked influence of Catholicism, which teaches that "Purgatory" exists. That is an imaginary place, sort of a half-Hell, invented by ancient Christian mythmakers as a destination after death for people who did not obey God in this life, but weren't all that bad. Therefore, that doctrine holds, they are rewarded with a second chance to go to Paradise, after they have been "purged" in Purgatory by suffering an appropriate length of time. But it is foolish to think that any amount of suffering on our part can purge our sins. Only the blood of Christ can do that for us, and no man of God has ever taught that after death, the sin-cleansing blood of Christ is still available to sinners.

Pastor John

===

Hello John,

Thank you for your message last night on "tartarization". I am thankful for some meat, John – meat that makes me lie on my bed at night and pray for God to help me, to have mercy on me, to help me love Him more, and to obey Him. Of course, it takes "doing", and for that, we have the power of the holy Ghost. Most of God's children do not have such a privilege to eat the food you feed us, John. I want to stay VERY thankful for being allowed at this table. May God bless all His children to hear the things from Him that we regularly hear through you.

John, Wendell's question and your answer brought some thoughts to me of these verses in 2Peter 3:9–11: "The Lord of the promise is not slow, as some think of slowness, but waits patiently for us, not wanting any to perish, but for all to come to repentance. But the day of the Lord will come like a thief in the night, in which the heavens will pass away with a roar, and the elements, consumed with burning heat, will be destroyed, and the earth and the works that are in it will be burned up. So then, seeing that all these things are to be destroyed, what kind of people ought *y*ou to be in all holy conduct and godliness?"

Just because God does not immediately strike us dead when we sin, or even when we are weak and sin multiple times, does not mean He is slack. It does not mean we have gotten by or that He does not consider it important.

But God's long-suffering is SO great and His offering of repentance is SO generous that it's hard to take in. But as Peter said, He is not slack, either. If correction comes time and time again, and we don't let the Spirit fix it, what will God's options be? Either death for our good (cf. 1Cor. 11:29–32) or tartarization, the living damnation.

My point is this: personally, since I have been in this truth, I have NEVER seen a situation where you had not been working to correct a person MANY times before God eventually sent them away somewhere (in their hearts first, and then, bodily). It is just as Peter said: God is long-suffering, "not willing that any should perish." But there does come a time. It is different with each person – a different level of patience and a different amount of time the door stays open.

But then, there is a time when it is over. When that time will be, only God knows. But it's not something to be played around with or delayed when correction comes our way. We need to fix it with all our heart, soul, AND BODY! We need to fix it FAST! What manner of people ought we to be in all holiness, godliness, and lifestyle, knowing the time WILL come?

Gary

Conclusion

One of the precious truths about Hell and the Lake of Fire which reveals the gospel to be wonderful news is that nobody has to go there. The essential element of the New Testament is that God sent His Son to die in our stead because He wants no one to perish, but that all might come to repentance (2Pet. 3:9). Jesus made the way for "whosoever will" to escape the damnation that awaits sinners, and every soul who ends up in the Lake of Fire will be forever tormented by the same thought: "I didn't have to be here!" That is the "worm" of regret which will never stop gnawing at tormented souls.

This is a book about the love of God as much as anything else, "for God so loved the world that He gave His only Son so that every one who believes in him should not perish but have eternal life" (Jn. 3:16). How glad we should be that Christ Jesus has provided a means of escape from the wrath to come and that in him, we find an acceptable way to live and worship God. When the Bible's message about Hell is rightly communicated, it reveals that although God is certainly austere and just, He also is long-suffering and merciful.

There are, as the Reader has seen, some unanswered and perhaps unanswerable questions concerning Hell and the other places we have discussed. Our purpose in this book, even though we cannot provide those answers, has been to benefit those who read it and to glorify God for His mercy. Hopefully, we have at least encouraged our Readers to "fear God and keep His commandments, for that," said wise Solomon, "is the whole duty of man" (Eccl. 12:13).

We will conclude with a comment from one of "the boys":

When we researched the question "Do people in Hell worship God?" we found out that they cannot. From Psalm 6:5, we read, "In death, there is no remembrance of you [God]; in [Hell], who shall give you thanks?" Wow.

So, my conclusion is that you should do all of your praising God while you are on earth, live right, and then, you will be able to praise God in Heaven with all the others who will be there. Then, you won't even have to worry about [Hell], much less the Lake of Fire.

Aaron Nelson

Appendix

Using Ancient Myths

Understandably, there have been questions raised as to the appropriateness of using material from ancient heathen mythology in such a study as this. My response is that I have found elements of truth, remnants of truth once revealed but then forgotten, imbedded in many ancient myths. I believe that the evidence shows a significant portion of the mythology of the ancient world had roots in revealed truth, but truth which had been twisted, grossly at times, by the vain imaginations of men.

For example, it is a known fact that stories of a worldwide flood are found in unconnected cultures all around the globe. It seems obvious that there had to have been a common basis for those flood stories and that the common basis for them was the truth about the Flood that is recorded in Genesis 7–9. I also believe that the non-biblical flood stories that existed in ancient heathen cultures were written after Noah's Flood and are perversions of that holy biblical story.

When Homer, Virgil, and other ancient poets and writers began their work, they would often begin with a prayer to the goddesses called Muses for revelation of the events they were about to relate and for aid in telling the story accurately and well. Inasmuch as Moses, Paul, and other godly men said that the gods of the Gentiles were in fact demons (e.g., Dt. 32:17; 1Cor. 10:20), I believe that these ancient poets were contacting real spiritual beings and that those spirits really did communicate historical truths to them – mixed, of course, with error. We know that demons can reveal otherwise unknowable information to humans, and even perform miracles through them; the Bible presents us with many examples, such as the fortune-telling slave girl in Philippi (Acts 16:16) and the Egyptian magicians in Exodus 7:11–12. Likewise, ancient poets, I believe, had a real connection with fallen angels – demons – who sometimes spoke to them, revealing elements of the hidden past and inspiring fanciful elaborations on it.

There was truth revealed to man that predated the myths of classical Greece, and once we learn the truth from Christ, we can discern the remnants of that truth in those myths. Pride, the product of carnal knowledge (1Cor. 8:1), tempts modern man to entirely dismiss the works of ancient poets as the childish fruit of an insufficiently evolved species. But history teaches us not to be quite so smug and skeptical. The ancients were not as ignorant and gullible as proud modern man would like to think. In the late 19th century, Heinrich Schliemann was ridiculed by some experts in classical history because of his opinion that Homer's epic, *The Iliad*, had a historical basis. When he set sail to search for ancient Troy, few expected him to discover it, confident as they were that Homer's entire story was a product of a fertile, unsophisticated human imagination. But when Schliemann, following Homer's detailed geographic information, discovered the ruins of the city of Troy in northwest Asia Minor, the entire scholarly world was stunned. Once again, declarations of scholars and experts were proved to have sand as their foundation. The pretensions of many scholars and experts were exposed, again, as based more on pride for what little they knew than on humility before God for their ignorance.

So, I believe that it is good to see and point out truth, or elements of it, regardless of where that truth is found. Doing so can add color to one's story and increase interest; it can give the Reader a wider and better perspective of the issues involved; and it can enlighten as to how certain matters developed. Admittedly, it can also at times turn out to be useless clutter, but I hope that I have avoided that pitfall.

The Spirits in Prison

Some scriptures related to Hell leave us with unanswered questions, to be sure. Some are added here so that the Reader may consider them. Perhaps the Lord will enlighten someone who reads this, who will then pass that understanding on to us.

Jesus said that after he died, he would be in "the heart of the earth" three days (Mt. 12:40), and while on the cross, he told the repentant thief who was crucified with him that he would that day be with him in Paradise (Lk. 23:43). Does that mean that Jesus only went to the Paradise portion of Hell? Certain prophecies about Jesus' descent into the heart of the earth suggest he went to the worst part of Hell, such as this, from Psalms: "You have set me in the lowest Pit, in the darkest of depths. Your burning anger pressed upon me; you overwhelmed me with all your waves" (Ps. 88:6–7). But, the lowest Hell seems to have been reserved for the wicked (cf. Ps. 63:9). There are some who teach that Jesus did go into Torment and suffer in those flames, but the Bible does not give us enough information to determine if that is true or not.

Peter said that when Jesus descended into Hell, he did so in order to preach "to the spirits in prison," and then he tells us who those people are: "who once were unbelieving, when in the days of Noah, the long-suffering of God waited while the ark was being prepared" (1Pet. 3:19–20). So, the spirits in prison to whom Jesus descended and preached are those who lived in Noah's day, that is, before Moses and the law. Of them, Paul wrote that "before the law, sin was in the world, but sin is not imputed when there is no law" (Rom. 5:13), which suggests that those who died before the law had not yet received their final judgment when Jesus came and preached to them. For those born under the law, Jesus said that Moses would be their judge (Jn. 5:45), so there was no point in Jesus preaching to them. Their judgment was set.

Jesus' story of Lazarus, the poor beggar who died and was taken by angels into the comfort of Abraham's bosom, has been a wonderful encouragement to the poor since Jesus told it, but it also raises a question. Lazarus lived and died under the law, but Abraham lived and died centuries before the law. Yet, they were together in Paradise. So, how did Jesus manage to preach to the one, Abraham, and not the other, Lazarus? He may have just told everyone there that his message was only for those who lived before Moses. And one would have expected to find those who lived before the law being kept in a different part of Hell from those who lived under the law, but Abraham and Lazarus are in the same place. Again, the Bible yields no resolution to those issues, and so we must leave it there. It is unwise to speculate about the things God has chosen to keep to Himself (cf. Dt. 29:29).

New Testament Mercy

The closest thing to one's sin being blotted out before Christ came was when God "put away" David's sins during his wretched affair with Bathsheba. That degree of mercy was not allowed by the law of Moses. It was a forgiveness completely unexpected because it was unlawful. It was a taste of New Testament mercy in an Old Testament setting, and it so confused and divided the Israelites that it led to civil war. One side was led by David's own son Absalom, who did not believe that God had shown such mercy to David. The other side, much smaller than the first, was made up of those who believed that God had done so, even though they, too, could neither understand nor explain it.

Tartarus

It is obvious from words that Homer placed on Zeus' lips that in ancient times, the Greeks believed in an extremely gloomy place, worse than Hell, which they called *Tartarus*. However, the fact that Peter knew and used the word *tartarus* (in verb form) does not mean that Peter was imitating Homer; rather, it means that there was a basis of truth behind some of Homer's work, truth that was perverted as generations of men fell more deeply into sin. Homer's mythological perversion of the truth about the existence of a place worse than Hell does not in the least make that place a myth. And Peter's use of the word *tartarus* does not mean that he was formulating doctrine based on heathen mythology. He was an anointed man of God moved by the Spirit of truth to write what he wrote. Knowing that some would think otherwise, however, Peter declared to his readers, "We did not follow cunningly fabricated myths when we made known to *y*ou the power and coming of our Lord Jesus Christ" (2Pet. 1:16).

Peter was moved by the Spirit of God to tell the unadulterated truth. Homer was moved by demons to fabricate myths, sprinkled throughout with vague remnants of truth that demons remembered or that God had revealed to men before Homer, but had been neglected by them and lost.

Fallen Angels

Much of what is said here concerning the place and status of fallen angels hinges on them being the demons mentioned throughout the Bible. The Bible never explicitly states that demons are the angels that fell, but there is evidence which strongly suggests it, such as the story in 1Kgs. 22:20–23. We also have Jesus' mention of "the Devil and his angels" (Mt. 25:41) and John's revelation that the Devil and his angels fought with the archangel Michael and his angels, and were defeated and cast out of Heaven (cf. Rev. 12:7–9; 20:2). One should note that the Bible never uses the word *rapture*, but there will be one. Nor does the Bible explicitly state that it was Satan who deceived Eve, but he did it. So, it seems clear, based on the biblical evidence, that the angels who were permanently cast out of Heaven after Jesus ascended are the demons mentioned throughout the Bible.

We lay a snare for our own feet when we insist that no truth exists unless it is plainly stated in the Bible. There is much truth that is not in the Bible. That is why we needed the Spirit; it alone is able to guide us into all truth; Jesus said so (Jn. 16:13). Led by the Spirit, Paul appealed to common sense (1Cor. 11:14), or offered his own judgment about a matter (1Cor. 7:6–7), for he had no scripture to use in order to prove his point, and the Spirit had not revealed anything to him about the matter at hand (cf. 1Cor. 7:39–40).

The Way of Balaam

"The way of Balaam" refers to the system of hiring ministers to teach what men want to hear. Jesus referred to such ministers as "hirelings" (Jn. 10:12–13). And Paul prophesied of the rise of this kind of ministry among believers: "The time will come when they will not put up with sound doctrine, but will heap up [hire] teachers for themselves according to their own lusts, having itching ears" (2Tim. 4:3). Peter's prophecy of false teachers among the saints concerned those ministers who would follow Balaam's example.

Though not an Israelite, Balaam served the true God, and he became famous for his many true prophecies. King Balak of Moab, hearing of Balaam, offered him great wealth if he would make the long trip south to Moab and prophesy against Israel. Balaam eventually went, but God would not allow him to curse His people, and so, Balak refused to pay Balaam. Frustrated at the lost opportunity for a big payday, Balaam consulted with nearby Midianites (the shrewdest people on earth), and they helped him devise a plan that would gain for Balaam the reward that Balak had offered. Balaam's plan for Balak was to conquer Israel with friendship,[20] not war, by blending with them through marriages and by joint worship of Israel's God and the gods of Moab. It was crafty advice, and when Israel fell into the pretty trap, Balak was pleased and Balaam secured his reward.

---

[20] To conquer God's children by peace is a cunning tactic that will one day be used again to entrap them (Dan. 8:25).

Balaam's crafty counsel to King Balak inflicted a deep wound on Israel's spirit which endured for centuries. It was one of the most treacherous acts ever by a servant of God. Balaam's sin was so grievous that Jesus was still speaking of it in the last book of the Bible (Rev. 2:14). Balaam rented himself out, so to speak. He labored to gain a reward from men instead of from God. Though a servant of God, Balaam became a "hireling", performing a religious service for money. This system of hiring a man to minister is seen today when religious sects hire men to minister to them according to their beliefs and practices. The most successful ministers within that system enthrall their audiences, but the thrill is not of God. For those who are newly converted to Christ, such ministers are an especially dangerous attraction (2Pet. 2:18b), for they appear to be leading souls to liberty, but they themselves have "returned to their own vomit" and are now "servants of corruption" (2Pet. 2:22, 19).

The Beast

Adolph Hitler serves as an example of how a world ruler could "die" without any actual proof of his death. All that was ever found of his body, according to Russian officials and documents, was the charred remains of a man about his size. Tests performed on bone fragments eventually made available to Westerners after the 1993 collapse of the Soviet Union indicated that the body which the Soviets had kept from the West was Hitler's. Therefore, it is possible that Hitler really did kill himself, as was claimed by the Soviets in 1945. On the other hand, it may be possible that the burned body they found in a shallow grave outside Hitler's bunker in 1945 was not that of Hitler.

I am not saying that Hitler is the Beast of Revelation; I am only using Hitler and his mysterious death as an example of how men may assume a death has taken place when it did not. At the same time, it is not only Hitler's death that serves as an example of the Beast, in how he will be able to reappear from the past, but also Hitler's savagery toward the Jews. He reflected very well Satan's deep hatred of them, which hatred the Beast, whoever he is, will also share.

An important element of the Beast's story is that when he returns to reign on earth again, *he will be recognized.* This could hardly be the case with any earthly ruler if he lived before the time when pictures or film were invented. If a man arose to power in the future and claimed to be an ancient Pharaoh returned to earth, he would immediately be dismissed as a lunatic. It would be impossible, even with the technology and information we have today, for him to prove his claim and convince the masses. But a more modern ruler would be easily recognizable to billions of people. Satellites and the media have made the faces of rulers familiar to people around the world. Again, for example, because of an obsession with Hitler on the part of book publishers, movie makers, etc., Hitler's face is arguably the most recognizable face of anyone who has ever walked the earth.

Whoever the Beast proves to be, he will be immediately recognizable to the world's inhabitants as someone who has previously lived and ruled on earth. He will be a well-known ruler from history who is presumed to be dead, but will reappear on the world stage, still lusting for earthly political power and still hating the Jews with all his heart.

Are You Ready for Jesus Not to Come?

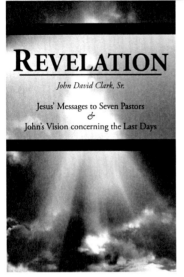

REVELATION

John David Clark, Sr.

Jesus' Messages to Seven Pastors
&
John's Vision concerning the Last Days

The question, "Are you ready for Jesus to come?" may be a good question to ask, but the more appropriate question is, "Are you ready for Jesus not to come?" because the reality is that it is not time for Jesus to return. So, the real issue is, are we ready to stay here and do the work that remains to be done? Are we prepared to endure what this world and the body of Christ will suffer before the coming of the Lord?

After examining the seven messages from Jesus to the pastors of seven congregations, this study of John's revelation reveals why the Jews rejected Jesus and presents in great detail the wonderful promises God made to Israel through the prophets, all of which will be fulfilled after He has greatly scourged and sifted the nation for their rebellion against Christ.

When Were the Disciples Born Again?

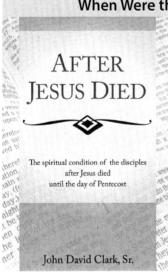

AFTER JESUS DIED

The spiritual condition of the disciples after Jesus died until the day of Pentecost

John David Clark, Sr.

If anyone on earth was born again after Jesus died, and before Pentecost, surely his disciples were - but they were not. If anyone on earth understood his purpose and doctrine after Jesus died, and before Pentecost, surely his disciples did - but they did not. *After Jesus Died* shows that the Bible leaves no reasonable alternative to those two conclusions.

When we carefully study the disciples' actions and words in the time between Jesus' death and the day of Pentecost, we are forced to conclude that they were not born again until they were baptized with the Spirit on Pentecost morning. May God give us the same grace that He gave to his disciples to escape spiritual blindness and to walk with Jesus in his light. "The God who commanded light to shine out of darkness has shone in our hearts to give us the light of the knowledge of the glory of God in the face of Jesus Christ."

Who told you that you were born again?

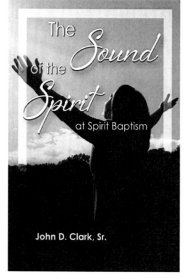

John D. Clark, Sr.

We need to know who has received the Spirit of God and who has not. Otherwise, we are lost in a world of religious confusion as to who really is born of God and who is not. This is the condition that exists among believers today.

The Sound of the Spirit at Spirit Baptism presents an accurate and consistent biblical explanation for the sound of the Spirit being the sign that one has been baptized by Christ with the holy Spirit. If true, this belief radically alters the commonly accepted picture of the body of Christ, for since the baptism of the Spirit is the only means of entering the body of Christ (1Cor. 12:13) then the body of Christ would be composed only of those who have received that baptism, with the audible evidence Jesus said would accompany that blessing.

Prophet to an Apostate Nation

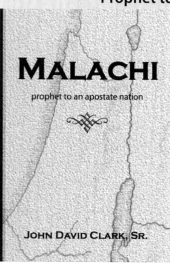

MALACHI

prophet to an apostate nation

JOHN DAVID CLARK, SR.

Malachi was a prophet who labored in a very dark time in Israel's history, and his answer to the darkness was the law of Moses - God's law. He pleaded with Israel to repent and live by that holy law, but the Israelites were indignant at Malachi's warnings. Ours is just such a dark time. The true word of God is rarely spoken, and when it is, it is often scorned. As the book Malachi amply shows, Jesus' comment concerning the path to eternal life, "few there be who find it," applied to ancient Israel as it does to us.

To persuade transgressors to repent and to exhort the faithful to be steadfast has been the task of God's servants throughout human history, whether they be the prophets of ancient Israel or God's ministers today. The true prophets in Israel were sent to point God's people to the way of His law, and God's true ministers today are sent to point His people to the way of His Spirit.

Books by John D. Clark, Sr.

——⟨⟩⟨⟩⟨⟩——

Spiritual Light

Suffering and the Saints

The Sound of the Spirit at Spirit Baptism

Holy Bible - Is It the Word of God?

Marriage and Divorce

Solomon's Wisdom

God Had a Son before Mary Did

Tithes and Offerings

Malachi

After Jesus Died

Revelation

The Iron Kingdom Book Series:
  Book 1: Slander
  Book 2: The Jerusalem Council
  Book 3: The Apostate Fathers

——⟨⟩⟨⟩⟨⟩——

For free book downloads visit us at:
www.GoingtoJesus.com